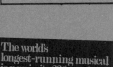

The Fantasticks

For B. Iden Payne

The original Sullivan Street cast, beginning clockwise, with HUGH THOMAS (Bellomy) in straw hat, TOM JONES (Henry) in mask, BLAIR STAUFFER (Mute) in top hat, JERRY ORBACH (El Gallo) in sombrero, JAY HAMPTON (Handyman) in glasses, KENNETH NELSON (Matt) in sweater, WILLIAM LARSEN (Hucklebee) in suspenders, GEORGE CURLEY (Mortimer) in feather, and RITA GARDNER (Luisa) standing in the center.

(Photo/Robert Benton)

The Fantasticks

ANNIVERSARY 30 EDITION

by TOM JONES and HARVEY SCHMIDT

With Special 30th Anniversary Foreword
and Illustrations by the Authors

APPLAUSE
THEATRE BOOK PUBLISHERS

211 West 71 St. New York, N.Y. 10023

Library of Congress Cataloging-in-Publication Data

Schmidt, Harvey.
   [Fantasticks. Libretto]
   The fantasticks / by Tom Jones and Harvey Schmidt : with special 30th
anniversary foreword and illustrations by the authors. — 30th anniversary
ed.
      p.   cm. -- (The Applause musical library)
   Discography: p.
   ISBN 1-55783-074-6 : $19.95
   1. Musicals -- Librettos. 2. Schmidt, Harvey.   Fantasticks.
I. Jones, Tom, 1928-   . II. Title. III. Series.
ML50.S347F42   1990   <Case>
782.1'4--dc20   90-33931
                                                          CIP

Applause Theatre Book Publishers
211 West 71st Street
New York, NY 10023
(212) 595-4735

First Applause Printing, 1990

Contents

1. Trying to Remember   1

- One Man's Recollections of the origins of *The Fantasticks* by TOM JONES

2. The Fantasticks   29

- Book and Lyrics by TOM JONES
- Music by HARVEY SCHMIDT
- Drawings by HARVEY SCHMIDT

3. A Scrapbook   113

- About the Authors
- About *The Fantasticks*
- "Abductions" (And So Forth)
- About the Producers
- Memorabilia
- Anniversaries
- Caricatures
- Recordings of the Music

1

Trying to Remember

One Man's Recollections of the Origins of THE FANTASTICKS

By Tom Jones

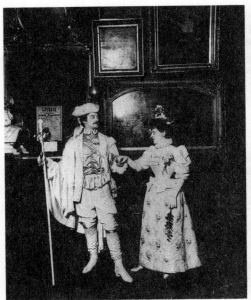

Scenes from the Comédie Française production of *Les Romanesques*.

"I tell the future. Nothing easier." So says the Fortune Teller in *The Skin of Our Teeth*. "But," she adds profoundly, "who can tell the past?"

Of that small handful of people who were involved in the original production of *The Fantasticks*, no two will remember it quite the same. Even Harvey and I, who were there at the very beginning, and who have, in tandem, answered the same questions about its history for fully thirty years — even we differ, on particulars if not on primary events.

This then is my own particular version of the story of *The Fantasticks*. It is not true history. It is personal reminiscence, as selective as that phrase implies, and also as flawed. Like Dylan Thomas who "plunged his hands" into the white snow of his childhood and came up with that Christmas in Wales, I sit now at my desk in Connecticut and try to summon up the past. — What do I remember? What images come forth to fill this empty page?

THE WRITING

Iden Payne. I suppose that is the first figure to emerge. B. Iden Payne. Professor of Drama at the University of Texas from 1946 to the late 1960s. Before that, he was—what? What was he *not*, in fact? A young actor in Benson's fabled Shakespearian company in England at the turn of the century. At twenty, a director at the Abbey Theatre (he arrived there the night of the *Playboy* riots and feared this was a typical Irish audience). Head of the Manchester Repertory. Director, in New York, of Otis Skinner and William Gillette and all those Barrymores. (He gave John Barrymore his first serious role, in Galsworthy's *Justice*.

He also gave fourteen-year-old Helen Hayes her first important part on Broadway, in *Dear Brutus*.) Let's see. What else? He started the first Drama Department in the United States, at Carnegie Tech. He was, briefly, head of the Stratford On Avon Theatre. He opened a replica of Shakespeare's theatre, called the Globe, at the Chicago World's Fair, and later became its mentor and frequent director when it moved to San Diego. He was an extraordinary man, a fine stage director and also a great, great teacher. It was my privilege to be his student from 1946 to 1951, when I finished my M.F.A. in Drama.

While I was in Mr. Payne's Period Play Production class, he introduced us to a rather obscure Rostand play called *Les Romanesques*. This charming, but trifling, piece, written when Rostand was twenty-four and played with modest success by the Comédie Française, had been adapted into English in 1900 by a woman writing under the pseudonym of George Fleming. It was done in London that same year with Mrs. Patrick Campbell playing the boy's role as a "breeches part." In 1907, Mr. Payne revived the piece when he was head of the Gaiety Theatre, Manchester. Some forty years later, he used a scene from this English adaptation (which, incidentally, was called *The Fantasticks*) for his graduate students. The scene, which each of us staged, was one in which the female Mr. Fleming had come up with the conceit of having the bandit Straforel describe his various abductions as "rapes," in the playful manner of *The Rape of the Lock*.

I could scarcely have guessed that this amusing little scene from this amusing little play would have a profound effect upon my life. I did not think of it as a possible source for a musical because I did not think of *anything* as a possible source for a musical. I was a director, not a writer. Certainly I was not a writer of musicals. I don't think I had ever seen a musical, except in the movies. Though we did literally hundreds of plays while I was at the University of Texas, we never did one single musical, not even Gilbert and Sullivan. It was only later, when I was in graduate school, doing extracurricular work in an organization called the Curtain Club, that I met Harvey Schmidt and Word (at that time, Charles) Baker, and we began to discover the exhilaration of the musical theatre.

Harvey and I wrote two college musicals together. The first, called *Hipsy-Boo!* (Yes, *Hipsy-Boo!*), was directed by Word Baker. The second, an annual production called *Time Staggers On*, was directed by me. Both were enormous hits, popular hits of the sort we had never encountered in the rarefied atmosphere of the classically minded Department of Drama. They were the sort of hits that sold out all the seats, and then the standing room, and then the aisles, and then, finally, the windows, where the chosen few would stand in clumps, looking into the theatre and reporting what was happening onstage to the people outside who couldn't see or hear anything at all.

This was heady stuff. So heady that, in spite of the fact that I was a Directing major and Harvey was an Art student, we continued to write songs together by long distance mail when first I, and then later, Harvey, were both drafted into the Army during the Korean War.

Since I went in first, I got out first. Soon after my release from the military, I went to New York, fully intending to become a director of plays (the more classical the better). Discovering quickly that my services as a director were not in demand, I decided to write comedy material while I waited for the "big break." I wrote an act for Tom Poston and Gerry Matthews, which led to Julius Monk and the world of supper club revues. Also, while waiting for Harvey to become a civilian again, I joined forces with a composer named John Donald Robb. Dr. Robb, a distinguished man who had been a successful lawyer, had always wanted to compose. While at Yale, in the same class as Cole Porter, he had played around with music. Later, after his entry into corporate law, he had studied composition with the famed Nadia Boulanger in Paris. And later still, when he retired, he settled near the University of New Mexico, where he promptly became head of the Music School and Dean of the College of Fine Arts. In 1955 he took a year's sabbatical with the specific goal of writing a musical comedy. He was introduced to me by someone at ANTA, and in short order we were having meetings, trying to select something to musicalize.

I truly do not remember which of us suggested the Rostand piece but, whatever the sequence, we soon decided this would make a "fun musical," and we set to work together. Our adaptation was called *Joy Comes to Deadhorse*. Why? I don't know why. I don't know why now, and I don't think I knew why then. Our musical was to be a Western, set in — where else? — Deadhorse. We relied as much or more on *Romeo and Juliet* as we did on *Les Romanesques*. Two ranches quarreling. One Spanish, the other Anglo. (This was before *West Side Story*.) The girl's father named Don Luis; her name therefore Luisa. The other rancher named Bellomy. Luisa had a nurse, a duena, just like Juliet. And to top it off, we even had a villain, modeled on Tybalt, who was a half-breed Apache.

Into this rather mixed bag, I added M. Rostand's bandit Straforel, now known as El Gallo (named after a famous gypsy bullfighter), plus two roly-poly sidekicks borrowed substantially from the Cisco Kid movies of my youth. And later, in the big abduction sequence, I threw in an old medicine show ham named Henry Fenwick.

Our work went well. That is to say, it was friendly and productive. I spent much of the summer as Dr. Robb's guest at his beautiful farm on Shelter Island and I glimpsed, for the first time in my West Texas life, the gracious living of the cultured Eastern establishment, a world of rambling homes and large families and friends coming over for cocktails and amateur string quartets. I was impressed. More than that, I was awed. This man was one of the finest and most cultured I had ever met, and our relationship quickly became that of surrogate father and son. If I had any doubts about the music, I quickly squelched them as disloyal and stupid. After all, the music *was* accomplished and, one might even say, classical. If it was a bit short on "show tunes," it did seem appropriate for the strange mixture of opera, operetta and Broadway we were trying to concoct.

In the spring of 1956, *Joy Comes to Deadhorse* had its premiere at the University of New Mexico. I was there for the rehearsals and for the opening and for the brief run. And despite the respectful response from the academic audience and the generally warm reception from the local press, I felt the whole thing was a mess, a totally hopeless mix of styles and intentions, with melodrama mixing queasily with whimsy and romanticism.

Dr. Robb felt differently. Despite a few minor flaws here and there, he perceived the piece as successful. There was no middle ground here. I felt it was *basically* wrong. He felt it was *basically* right. So we split. I gave him the rights to anything I had written for it, and he gave me the right to pursue it in another version, with another composer, who turned out to be Harvey Schmidt.

Harvey and I worked on our version of *Joy* for about three years. And we floundered. Never did it occur to us to question the basic premise; i.e. "can a charming little whimsical play be made into a big cowboy musical, written for Broadway in the Rodgers and Hammerstein manner?"

Finally it all collapsed. A couple of songs were pretty good. A few speeches were not without charm. But the *premise* was wrong. It was structurally unsound. Strange, I had seen this so clearly when I had worked with Dr. Robb, but I had fallen into exactly the same traps when I began working with Harvey. I couldn't seem to change it. I didn't know how. If not Rodgers and Hammerstein, then what? There was nothing else. Virtually all musicals at that time were patterned after the R & H mold. And a good and useful pattern it was, too. It produced most of the great American musicals. Nevertheless, it was, quite simply, unworkable for *Les Romanesques*. And finally even Harvey and I were ready to give up.

Then several seemingly unrelated things happened in quick succession. First of all, my father died. He died, unexpectedly, at the age of fifty-eight, and he died in debt. I had never, since college, relied upon financial help from home, but at the same time my needs were modest, and I lived a careless, carefree, essentially adolescent life, a life without much responsibility or sense of direction. Now it was different. It had to be. My mother was left without any money or visible means of support. In time she could, and would, get a job. In the meantime, I had to help. No longer could I afford to go for years "playing at" being a writer, doing a few scenes and songs each year on a seemingly hopeless project. It was, as they say in the South, time to fish or cut bait.

The second unexpected factor was Harvey's sudden availability. He had come to New York as a commercial artist and he had prospered, working first for NBC television and then branching out to do more and more magazine assignments. Now, with money saved and his future promising, he decided to take off from his art assignments for a year to work with me full-time on our musical theatre endeavors. And I must add, without this rather courageous and generous gesture, *The Fantasticks* would never have come to be.

The third factor, which turned out to be the catalyst, was Word Baker, our director from the old University of Texas days. In the spring of 1959, Word got a job as the director of three original one act plays to be presented at the Minor Latham Auditorium at Barnard College in New York, where Mildred Dunnock was to produce a season of summer stock. Word wanted to make one of these one acts a musical, so he came to us with a proposal: if we could take our floundering *Deadhorse*, reduce it in size, and have it ready to show to Millie Dunnock in one month, he would guarantee us a production one month after that.

So, suddenly, it all came together. We threw out the R & H model. We gratefully let go of our adjoining ranches and our chorus of cowboys. We threw away the entire script and score, except for a couple of songs. We decided to break all the rules. We didn't understand them anyway. For years both Word and I had championed the idea of an "open stage," a presentational theatre which would exalt in theatrical devices rather than trying to hide them. This is what we would attempt. We would take all the things we liked about the theatre and try to throw them into one little one-act musical. After all, it was just for one week of summer stock. What did we have to lose?

These, as I said, were the three major events which came together to start *Les Romanesques* on its altered path to *The Fantasticks*. In addition, there were several other occurrences which were almost as important. First, there was *The Fantasticks*, the 1900 adaptation of the Rostand play by "George Fleming." By sheer accident, I happened to find it in the New York Public Library. I had never read it before, only the one or two scenes we had done in Mr. Payne's class. I was charmed. It had five characters, plus a few "supers" for the abduction. It was concocted in rhymed couplets, in the French manner. It had one set. It seemed to be a perfect role model for our little one act.

There were many changes, of course. More changes than similarities, as it turned out. First of all, there is nothing presentational at all about the George Fleming adaptation or the Rostand original. The setting is realistic, two adjoining gardens with a stone wall between them. There are no soliloquies. There is no direct address to the audience. There is no narrator, no mute, no cardboard moon, no sprinkled rain or snow. There are no old actors. There is no "freezing" of the action. And of course there are no songs. Even the basic point is different. At the end of the Rostand, in the one presentational moment, the girl, Sylvette, comes forward and addresses the audience, asking them to turn their backs on these dreary realistic plays invading the stage and seek instead for gossamer and romance. The point of our own version is that one must give up one's youthful illusions and romanticism and move into the season of maturity and reality.

Even so, even though the style and the very point of view of our musical was to be different from the original, the plot was to remain substantially the same. I determined to keep that little library book close by my side, and whenever I became hopelessly lost in my own verbiage and inventiveness, to turn back to the source to find my way out of the forest. And that, indeed, is what I did. I had rented Barbara Barrie's apartment for the summer while she was off in Stratford, "doing" Shakespeare. And every morning, dim and early, I worked. I say "dim" because when I worked it was not yet "bright." I had a job stage managing a Julius Monk revue called *DemiDozen*, which Harvey and I had substantially written, and every morning, around two, when the last lonely drinkers had departed, the staff — the waiters, performers, cooks and stage manager — all shared a huge meal together with whatever was left over from the kitchen. Then, around 4:00 a. m., I would go back to my little sublet on 28th Street, lay out a clean pad of paper, and as the sun was coming up over Bellvue, I would let my fancy take flight.

And flight it took. After years of relentless, wearisome struggling on the stillborn Western, now words — and scenes — and characters — came popping out, delighting and surprising me every morning.

Since I am putting all of this down in detail for the first and probably the only time, I would like to mention a few other sources which influenced *The Fantasticks*. I had just acquired a book by Harley Granville-Barker called *On Dramatic Method*, all about how Shakespeare achieved his dramatic effects, and I decided to use our little one act to experiment with some of the techniques. Shakespeare always had a unifying "palette" as well as a basic theme for each of his plays. For example, images of darkness abound in *Macbeth*, more than twice as many as in any other of his plays. Images of moonlight glue *A Midsummer Night's Dream* together. And so forth. Subtly, without making a big deal about it, the playwright surrounds you with an interconnected web of images which inform and unify the whole.

I decided, with *The Fantasticks*, to use images of vegetation and the seasons as the cohesive "code." When I was still in college, Christopher Fry announced that he was writing four plays, one for each of the seasons, and for some reason, I was very struck by that. When Harvey and I began writing revue material in New York, I found myself, over and over, coming up with lyrics or "poems," a strange sort of hybrid "spoken lyric" over music, about the seasons. It was very natural for us to transfer this to *The Fantasticks*, and it seemed justified by the garden setting of the original.

In addition to the unifying imagery, I studied Granville-Barker carefully for his analysis of Shakespeare's other "techniques" — the uses of rhymed verse and blank verse and prose and couplets to close scenes, etc. And I decided to attempt to write the dialogue in various forms of verse and, further, to stop upon occasion for a spoken aria, a lyrical passage of heightened images spoken over music.

There were lots of other influences on the piece from a variety of sources. Thornton Wilder's *Our Town*, with a narrator capable of stopping the action and moving us to and fro at will. The Piccolo Teatro di Milano had just been to New York with their brilliant production of Goldoni's *The Servant of Two Masters*, done in Commedia style with a platform and a company of actors who sat on the sidelines when not actually up on the platform stage. That had a profound impact on all of us. John Houseman's production of *A Winter's Tale* at Stratford, Connecticut, with its cold moon-like first act and its sun-drenched second, helped guide us to our cardboard sun and moon. Bernstein's original version of *Candide* (brilliant — much better than the later, more acclaimed, mutants) had opened its second act with heat and sour disgruntled "stings" of music. We borrowed from him as others have borrowed from us. (The opening of the second half of *Sunday in the Park with George*, with its characters all trying to maintain a happy, frozen, pose in the uncomfortable heat, is exactly like the opening of the second act of *The Fantasticks*.)

One last little admission of indebtedness. In a late forties movie called *A Double Life*, Ronald Coleman plays an actor who gets so caught up in the role of Othello that he commits murder and then later stabs himself on-stage. As he is dying, he tells of an old actor in England who specialized in death scenes and who was so successful that the audience would cry out "Die again! Die again!!" This brief mention, which I didn't consciously recall until we had been running for years, was, of course, the inspiration for Mortimer. It had come from the subconscious as, indeed, had come his name. Mortimer: Death. I swear to God I had no thought of this when I wrote the part. Things "happen" for you, or they don't. After years of struggling unsuccessfully, it suddenly all happened for us. *The Fantasticks* came pouring out without a struggle or a thought or even a re-write. As I was to discover later (sooner), this does not always happen.

Harvey tells a story about the music for "Try To Remember" which I am sure is the gospel truth. Being too poor at that time to own a piano, he had rented a small rehearsal studio and was trying to compose something, something complex and frustrating and elusive. Finally, he decided to stop and give himself a rest. And so he sat at the piano and played "Try To Remember," the complete melody, and all of the chords and even the key change at the end. It just poured out, a gift from some mysterious muse of music. And he thought: "My God, that's pretty." And so he played it again, and he put it on his tape machine to make sure it wouldn't get lost. A good deal of *The Fantasticks* came about exactly like that.

GETTING IT ON

During the summer of 1959, we played some six or seven songs for Mildred Dunnock on an old piano in a rehearsal studio at Barnard College, and we gave her a copy of the script, which was almost finished. She, in turn, gave us the go-ahead, and we set about completing the book and score in a couple of weeks so they could put it into rehearsal. We were supposed to use the acting company to fill all the roles, with the exception of Luisa. The singing was too difficult for any of the girls in the resident company so we auditioned and cast a vivacious and talented eighteen year old named Susan Watson. Though still quite young, she had experience in some of the big summer musicals, and she had just returned from the London production of *West Side Story*, where she had danced in the chorus and understudied Maria. In addition to being a terrific dancer, she was a classically trained singer, and the difficult obbligatos and the wide range and high notes presented no problem.

The other actors, as I said, came from the resident company. And they were good. We were lucky, luckier than we realized at the time. Jonathan Farwell played El Gallo, and he was tall, dark and reasonably dangerous, with a good singing voice and a fine command of the spoken verse. Ron Liebman played one of the Fathers and he was fine too, although he spent much of his time complaining about the frivolity of musicals in general and this musical in particular. Rolling his eyes heavenward and shaking his head, he would repeat, over and over: "This is not my kind of theatre." One of the actors, the young student who played Mortimer, was named Bill Tost. Decades later he joined *The Fantasticks* downtown at Sullivan Street, where he has played the Girl's Father brilliantly for years.

Physically, the production at Barnard was modest, but effective. The set, a platform with four poles, was based on sketches done by Harvey for a revue which he and Word and I were never able to get produced.

The Barnard Summer Theatre

presents

3

PREMIERES

THE FANTASTICKS
by TOM JONES and HARVEY SCHMIDT

THE MALL
by WILLIAM INGE

THE GAY APPRENTICE
by JACK DUNPHY

August 4-8, 1959

MINOR LATHAM PLAYHOUSE
BROADWAY AT 119TH STREET

"A Summer Theatre on Broadway"

Executive Director: MILDRED DUNNOCK   *General Manager:* DOLPH SWEET

Program cover for the bill of one acts at Barnard which introduced *The Fantasticks*.

(Photo/Henry Grossman)

Cast of the very first one-act version of *The Fantasticks* presented at Mildred Dunnock's Barnard Summer Theatre, August 1959. Left to right: GEORGE MORGAN, DICK BURNHAM, LEE CROGHAN, SUSAN WATSON, JONATHAN FARWELL, CRAYTON ROWE, RON LEIBMAN, BILL TOST.

The costumes, by Charles Lane (later Charles Blackburn, our design-er at Portfolio), were charming: a mixture of many theatrical styles from many theatrical eras. They were more "period" than our later production at Sullivan Street, more "commedia," more "faerie tale."

We had one week of rehearsal, if I remember correctly, running con-currently with the rehearsals for the other two one acts. One of those was *The Mall*, by William Inge. The other was *The Gay Apprentice* by Jack Dumphy. Our show was to open the bill. Harvey played the piano, a stolid upright positioned at the side of the stage, facing "up" with his back to the audience. Our choreographer, Lathan Sanford, was an ex-student of Word's who was in New York for the summer. Our stage manager was Geoffry Brown, who was later to fill the same position so capably at Sullivan Street. That's about all I can remem-ber. Danny Selznick ran the lights. I do recall that.

Fortunately for us, *The Fantasticks* broke down into many solo and duo "turns," which made rehearsal somewhat easier, but even so, we were under-prepared. Doing a new musical, even a one-act musical, simply takes more time than we had. And before we knew what had hap-pened, it was time for a run-through and then a preview and then an opening. Our running dates were August 4 through August 8; after that, the summer stock season went grinding on.

At our first run-through, our first time in the theatre, we had a trauma. Susan Watson lost her voice. She could speak. Barely. A hoarse, Tallullah-like whisper not at all appropriate for Luisa. She could not sing at all, not without the risk of destroying her vocal chords completely for the opening and the brief run. What to do? It was decided that Harvey would sing her songs for her and she would mouth the words. But that wasn't all. She had also fallen from a ladder and severely bruised her ribs. She could not dance. What to do? Of course. Our choreographer would dance for her. After all, it was only a run-through.

It was at exactly that moment that Lore Noto walked into our lives. He appeared, uninvited as far as I could tell, and not only that, he ap-peared with his lawyer, Donald Farber. He had come to see the show, possibly with the object in mind of producing it. I was livid. Who was this man? How did he get here? I tried to explain that this was our first run-through and, furthermore, our leading lady was ill, and the show was not going to be seen in its final form, and we were not ready for the pressure of an audience and, all things considered, it would be better if Mr. Noto took his lawyer and departed, perhaps returning when the show was actually finished and ready to be seen and judged.

Noto smiled tolerantly. He was wearing a white linen suit and a panama hat. He looked every inch the impresario. And he was not to be moved. Go on, he said, it's all right. He would make allowances. He knew all about rehearsals. Then, with Word's blessing, he was allowed to stay. (I was to learn later that Lore's determination was not easily to be deflected. His obstinacy, which then, and later, infuriated me, has been a major factor in the survival of *The Fantasticks*.)

What he saw was strange indeed. Every time our young heroine came to a musical number, she would open her mouth and a man's voice with a decidedly Texas twang would seem to emanate from her entrails. Every time she was supposed to dance, a muscular young man in blue jeans would leap into motion.

Lore loved it. It was, he said, a work of genius. He believed in it totally, almost mystically, and he never wavered, not through the long, difficult time of trying to raise money, not through the mixed notices, not through the nearly empty houses, not through the proposed closing. He was, and is, as you may surmise, a man of strong convictions and fixed ideas. This is sometimes extremely difficult to deal with, but ultimately, it was what we needed to get us launched.

We didn't, however, recognize that at the time. At the end of our brief run at Barnard, we had two other offers from producers who wanted to present our musical Off Broadway. One was from someone who wanted to keep the musical in its one act form, and combine it with some of our revue material. The other offer was from a man who wanted to expand the musical into a full evening, but who was not willing to pay us an advance. (Harvey and I decided that, no matter what happened, we would not let anyone produce the show who was not willing to gamble some sort of advance, however modest.)

Lore offered a combination of the two. He wanted the piece made into a full length musical, and he was willing to pay each of us 250 dollars as an advance against future royalties. Even so, we hesitated. Lore had only produced once, a play called *The Failures*, which closed after one performance. The other two producers had better track records. Then, in an effort to resolve the impasse, Lore met with Harvey, Word and me, and offered to write a clause into the contract saying that he would give the three of us complete freedom to make all artistic decisions, stepping in only if we were hopelessly deadlocked. That did it. With such an assurance of good faith, we signed a contract, took our 250 dollars each, and began to expand our musical into two acts while at the same time trying to help Lore Noto raise the proposed 16,500 dollars needed to capitalize the show.

We had thought, judging from the nifty summer suit and the panama hat and the vaguely eccentric manner (and the presence of a real, live lawyer), that Mr. Noto was some sort of eccentric millionaire who could simply write out a check for the production. This was not the case. The raising of that seemingly small sum took months of hard work and relentless backer's auditions. (It wasn't until later, much later, that we realized that Lore had quit his job and put up his entire life's savings of three thousand dollars to get the show launched.)

Beginning in October of 1959, we started doing a series of backer's auditions in an attempt to raise the money to present *The Fantasticks* Off Broadway. It was not an easy "sell." The first two or three auditions were fairly elaborate affairs held in the Cherry Lane Theatre with Susan Watson called in to help Harvey and me sing the score, and with large groups of potential backers in attendance. The results were disappointing. I don't know how much money was actually raised, but I do know that it wasn't nearly enough. Soon the extra expense of theatre rental and female singer were deemed too costly, with the result that for the next two months Harvey and I gave a series of auditions, unaided, in our apartment, for small handfuls of people who seemed as mystified by the whole procedure as we were. On one occasion a nice suburban couple dropped off an elderly lady, telling her, "All right, Mama. We'll be back to pick you up as soon as our movie is over." Then they left, and Harvey and I sang. and acted out the complete *Fantasticks* for the bewildered matron, who responded by smiling wanly and then drifting off to sleep.

In January of 1960, Lore made the decision to take in Associate Producers to help raise the money. In February, we held more elaborate backer's auditions at the Sullivan Street Playhouse, which belonged to one of our roommates, Bob Gold. And finally, at long, long last, the money was raised and a production was scheduled for the spring.

The other auditions, the ones where actors auditioned for us, were held in the apartment on 74th Street which Harvey and I shared with two other roommates. Actors lined up in the stairwell on the second and third floors and waited in the front hall until they were finally ushered into the living room to sing for Word, Harvey, Lore and myself, seated some four or five feet away. It was painfully proximitous for both actors and us, but as it turned out, these close quarters proved to be an apt approximation of the Sullivan Street Playhouse where it was finally decided, after much reluctance, that the show would be housed.

Jerry Orbach was the first one cast. He sang and read for us in the apartment, and before he could make his way down the stairs to the street, we had chased after him and offered him the role. The fathers came next: Bill Larsen, whom we had known since Texas days, and Hugh Thomas, who had written several musicals, but who also made an occasional stage appearance. For the young lovers, Word lined up several groups of possibilities and had them read and sing together. As Harvey wisely observed then (and later), you can't tell if people's heads are the same size unless you see them side by side. The two we chose were Rita Gardner and Kenneth Nelson, who performed and sang brilliantly, and whose heads were the same size. The second couple, who were almost as good, were Maureen Bailey and Ken Kerchival, later to go on to fame and fortune as one of the leads in the TV series *Dallas*. (In case you're wondering, Susan Watson was, by this time, playing the ingenue lead in *Bye, Bye, Birdie* on Broadway.)

(Photo/Robert Alan Gold)

Director WORD BAKER (center) rehearsing TOM JONES (left) and JERRY ORBACH (right) in the upstairs lobby at the Sullivan Street Playhouse in April, 1960.

Left: A quick sketch made by TOM JONES while he was suddenly having the idea that the Old Actor could appear from the prop trunk, during a meeting with WORD BAKER and HARVEY SCHMIDT that had been called to try and solve this entrance dilemma.

Below: TOM JONES, under the pseudonym of THOMAS BRUCE, emerging from the trunk as Henry, the Old Actor, in the original production.

(Photo/Freidman-Abels)

For the Indian, we cast George Curley, our stage manager at Julius Monk's. For the Old Actor, Henry, we could find no one. I had wanted Ellis Rabb, but he was off in Bermuda starting the APA company, which was later to take Broadway by storm. When rehearsals began and we still hadn't found anyone, I "read in" the part and eventually wound up opening in the role under the assumed name of Thomas Bruce. (Ironically, the fictional Mr. Bruce fared better in the reviews than the real Mr. Jones.)

THE OPENING

In April we rehearsed, first at the apartment on 74th Street and then at the Sullivan Street Playhouse. And then on May 3rd, 1960, we opened.

What do I remember about the opening? Everything. Nothing. There was a keen air of anticipation mixed with the usual butterflies and in my case, abject terror. We had done a week of previews, attended principally by people from the theatrical community, and these had gone well. As for me, I didn't know what to expect. I thought the piece was brilliant. Yes, I must admit it. That's exactly what I thought. Brilliant and personal and full of experiments never before attempted in a musical. *The Fantasticks* was one of a kind. It was not like any other. If I were to have hazarded a guess, I would have said that the critics would probably like it, but that it would be too offbeat to attract a large public. A success d'estime. Yes. I was quite prepared to settle for that.

The opening night performance did not go well. It did not go badly, but it did not go well. Compared with the week of previews, it was pale indeed. The Sullivan Street Playhouse is tiny, only 152 seats, and in those days the critics did not space out their coverage during final previews. They all came on opening night, and they wrote their reviews immediately after rushing out to waiting taxis, and the success or failure of this one performance would determine the success or failure of the show itself. Since there were so few seats available, there was no room (or, at least, not much) for backers and friends. Almost the entire audience was made up of somber, stony faces sitting in critical judgement.

I didn't see their faces, of course. At first, I was off-stage putting on my makeup for the Old Actor. Then I was on my knees, crouched in the dark entrails of the large Prop Trunk from which I was to make my entrance. And then finally I was on the stage itself, my poor myopic eyes blinded by the stage lights and scarcely able to see the other actors, much less the audience. But I could sense the audience; I could "feel" them. And it was not fun. Lines which had elicited roars only the night before now were met with silence or, at best, a few muffled chuckles. There was no Give and Take. No Ying and Yang. No Tossing It Back And Forth, which is the very essence of live comedy.

And to top it off, there was a disturbance during the middle of the first act. Crouched there, bent over double in my coffin-like Trunk, I could hear, just barely, hoarse shouting and some sort of scuffle. Later I discovered that one of the lesser critics had brought a date who was drunk, and during the middle of the act she began to mutter, rather like Tallullah in *The Skin of Our Teeth*, "Hey, what the hell is this? I don't know what this goddam thing is about!" The scuffling noise was the sound of the usher and the embarrassed critic trying to get her out of the auditorium, which at the Sullivan Street Playhouse meant dragging her across the front of the stage, amidst the actors.

They say in bullfighting that there are good bulls and bad bulls. The good bulls come at you. They play the game. They form a rhythm with the fighter. The bad bulls pull back. They find a safe, dark place, a "querencia," and they wait. And if you try to move them from this safe place, you are very likely to get gored.

Our opening night was like that.

The party was held at the spacious apartment of Ed Wittstein, our designer. Joanna Baker, Word's wise wife, had prepared huge heapings of delicious Mexican food, and there was abundant booze and beer. (It was on that night and at that party that I learned never to eat Mexican food at an opening.)

Around midnight it happened. A call came from the office of Harvey Sabinson, our press agent, and Word relayed the review out loud exactly as it was read to him over the phone. It was Brooks Atkinson. *The New York Times*.

I am looking at this review now. I have it, old and faded, unfolded upon my desk. It smells of age — not unpleasant, just musty. It is not bad. The music is "captivating" and "the style is entrancing." The first act is "fresh and sweet in a civilized way." But the review begins by saying that "two acts are one too many to sustain the delightful tone of the first." And it ends by saying "perhaps *The Fantasticks* is by its nature the sort of thing that loses magic the longer it endures."

Somehow, that night, read over the phone in sepulchral tones, it sounded like Doomsday. All we could hear, any of us, were the bad parts. Act Two is dull. That is not a survival notice.

Before we had time to assimilate this shock, the *Tribune* review by Walter Kerr was read. It was both better and worse. The first five paragraphs were an absolute rave for Jerry Orbach. The next was a rave for the nonexistent Thomas Bruce. There followed strong notices for the rest of the actors and then, in conclusion, this: "*The Fantasticks* does not hold its mannered head aloft for the full run of the book or the somewhat better score. It attracts you, settles back a bit limply, wakes you up again, and averages out a little less than satisfactory."

There it was. Mixed notices from both Atkinson and Kerr. Not bad notices. Full of much praise. But by no means enough to send anyone out to buy a ticket.

Of course, there were other daily papers at that time. John McClain, writing for the *Journal American*, headlined "*Fantasticks* a Delight," and said "It is wonderfully well suited to the small environs of the Sullivan Street Playhouse and should enjoy a long and lively occupancy." In the *New York Post*, Richard Watts, Jr. opined that "it has a freshness, youthful charm and a touch of imagination," but quibbled about "its lack of consistent effectiveness." Frank Ashton, in the *World Telegram and Sun*, called it a "musical pip," and reports he went home humming a new song called "Try To Remember."

These were the afternoon papers. They helped to soothe the hangovers of the next day. But meanwhile, back at the party, depression and near-hysteria had taken hold. No one knew what the afternoon papers would be, but everyone knew that the *Times* and *Tribune* were the ones that really mattered.

The party was over. Our press people advised Lore to close. Then. That night. By posting the notice right away, he could avoid paying an extra week's salary to the actors. But Lore was stubborn. He said no, let's wait for the other papers. And when they came in, he said no, let's wait for the magazines. He had total faith. He had burned his bridges. This had to succeed. It simply *had* to. And he had saved a few thousand dollars from the budget to tide us over, at least for a few weeks.

The magazines and the weeklies were good, almost uniformly so. Glover, of the Associated Press, called it "A sheer delight." Emory Lewis, in *Cue* magazine, said: "Bravo! The most inventive music in town! The brightest young talents now on display." Henry Hewes of the *Saturday Review* called it "A Magickal Musickal," noting that "Tom Jones and Harvey Schmidt have worked with a professional expertness equaling the best Broadway has to offer and with a degree of artistic taste that Broadway seldom attains any more." For some reason I don't have a copy of Edith Oliver's review in *The New Yorker*, but I do remember that it was good.

My favorite was by Michael Smith, writing for the *Village Voice*. Let me quote him:

"I am sadly out of practice at writing raves. As any critic knows, it is far easier to pick out a production's faults than its virtues, and I am hard pressed to explain *The Fantasticks*. With this in mind, I did something for the first time last week. Having seen the show free on Tuesday, its opening night, I bought tickets and went back on Thursday."

Then he goes on to summarize the plot, and points out that "the most elaborate and sophisticated art is employed to catch the audience in its simplicity. There is a breath-taking balance between worldly wit and commitment to naiveté." Then finally he concludes: "*The Fantasticks* is not the dregs of an uptown backers audition, nor an under-produced Broadway musical. What are usually limitations Off Broadway become advantages. I just might go see it again."

Mr. Smith, wherever you are in this wicked world, I salute you. A "balance between worldly wit and naiveté." Yes, that's it. That's what we wanted: to celebrate romanticism and mock it at the same time. To touch people, and then to make them laugh at the very thing that touched them. To make people laugh, and then to turn the laugh around, find the other side of it. To put two emotions side by side, as close together as possible, like a chord in music.

It's a strange thing about time. If you live a long time, you see the most unlikely things occur. And *The Fantasticks* has lived a long time. Four of those seven newspapers which reviewed us are now gone (more's the pity) as is *Cue* (consumed and condensed into a brief section of *New York Magazine*). The *Village Voice*, which praised us when we opened, some ten years later, in a follow-up review, said *The Fantasticks* is like a greasy MacDonalds hamburger, hard to digest and totally devoid of nutritional value. And a few years after that, the same *Village Voice* awarded the show an Obie for its distinguished contribution to Off Broadway.

Paper bullets. Words. Opinions this way, opinions that. Perceptive comments. Stupid evaluations. In time they are all reduced to their appropriate proportions. But in the beginning, they are Life and Death, at least in the theatre. And in our beginning the shadow of those first reviews loomed largely on our horizon.

Lore had saved some money from the budget. He was willing to gamble, especially after the afternoon papers and weekly reviews. Our running expenses were small, our theatre rental reasonable. It was worth "having a bash." And that is what we did.

Oh, the small houses! Oh, the empty seats! Even in our tiny theatre, there were never enough people to fill the small center section, much less the two sides. But we persevered, and slowly — oh, so slowly — it began to change. Some people did read those weeklies and in time (for, after all, it does take time to decide to make the effort) some of these people came down on a Saturday night or a Sunday. And these people liked it. And they began to tell other people.

Later that summer an unusual thing took place. For the first time since they had organized a union in the early part of the century, the Broadway actors went out on strike. It didn't last long, but it did have an impact on *The Fantasticks*. First of all, for that brief period, Off Broadway was the only show in town and that, of course, helped business. More important than that, all of the Broadway theatre people were suddenly free to go see other shows, and they came flocking to *The Fantasticks*.

And then a glittering period began. Our houses, though still small, were filled with luminaries, some of them legendary. Not only Richard Rodgers and Jerome Robbins and Gower Champion, but David Selznick and Vivien Leigh and Sir John Gielgud. And on and on and on. Myrna Loy. Henny Youngman. Anna May Wong. You name it.

Some people, like Anne Bancroft and Cheryl Crawford, became champions for the show, actually making out lists and calling people, telling them to go see it.

ANNE BANCROFT, an early supporter of the show, at the 100th Performance Party around the piano singing the show's songs with HARVEY SCHMIDT and TOM JONES.

At the end of the summer, Lore received an invitation from the John Drew Theatre in East Hampton to bring the show out there for two weeks. Acting again against the best advice of the "pros," Lore closed the production in New York, and off we went, trouping to the Hamptons. There we had a great success and, more to the point, we were discovered by the Hamptons crowd, the "in" crowd, the people who were the movers and shakers, the opinion makers.

Right after we returned, following the Labor Day weekend, a wonderful thing took place. We made a profit, a substantial one. We were not sold out, but almost. For the first time there was the contractual bonus for the actors, which was paid when the show went above a certain figure. No more the thirty-seven dollars and fifty cents take-home! I don't remember exactly what the new figure was, but it was over fifty dollars, and we were in Heaven.

The following week, the Sunday *New York Times* featured a picture of *The Fantasticks* along with a highly complimentary article by John Gassner, the eminent teacher and theatre historian.

And then we "settled in" for a run. A pattern developed, which stayed the same for a long time: modest houses on weekdays, sell-outs for the weekend. Nothing fancy. No "smash hit." But steady business, with good word of mouth. And before you knew it — before we knew it — it was our first birthday. And then our second.

It was a miracle. We had survived.

West Cornwall, Connecticut
February 1990

2

The Fantasticks

Book and Lyrics by
TOM JONES

Music by
HARVEY SCHMIDT

Suggested by a play
LES ROMANESQUES
by Edmund Rostand

Drawings by Harvey Schmidt

Original Cast

The Fantasticks was first presented by Lore Noto at the Sullivan Street Playhouse, New York City, on May 3rd, 1960, with the following cast:

THE MUTE.......................... Richard Stauffer

EL GALLO ....Jerry Orbach

LUISA .... Rita Gardner

MATT ....Kenneth Nelson

HUCKLEBEE .... William Larsen

BELLOMY..............................Hugh Thomas

HENRY....................................Thomas Bruce

MORTIMER .... George Curley

THE HANDYMAN...................Jay Hampton

* * *

THE PIANIST ....Julian Stein

THE HARPIST........................ Beverly Mann

Directed by WORD BAKER
Musical Director and Arrangements by
JULIAN STEIN
Production designed by ED WITTSTEIN

Associate Producers
SHELLY BARON, DOROTHY OLIM,
ROBERT ALAN GOLD

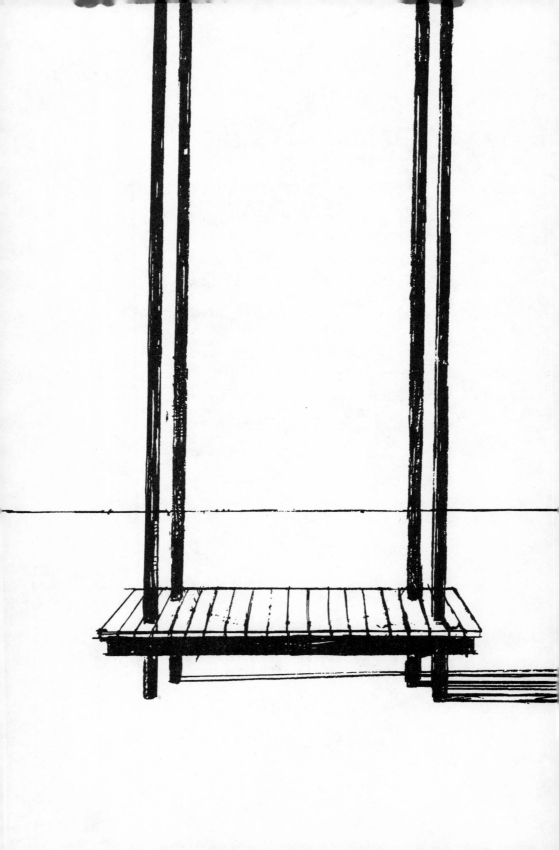

Musical Numbers

Act One

OVERTURE .... The Company

TRY TO REMEMBER... El Gallo

MUCH MORE .... Luisa

METAPHOR...Matt and Luisa

NEVER SAY "NO" ....Hucklebee and Bellomy

IT DEPENDS ON WHAT YOU PAY .... El Gallo,
Bellomy, and Hucklebee

SOON IT'S GONNA RAIN ....Matt and Luisa

THE RAPE BALLET .... The Company

HAPPY ENDING........................... Matt, Luisa, Hucklebee
and Bellomy

Act Two

THIS PLUM IS TOO RIPE ....Matt, Luisa,
Hucklebee and Bellomy

I CAN SEE IT .... El Gallo and Matt

PLANT A RADISH ....Hucklebee and Bellomy

ROUND & ROUND........... El Gallo, Luisa and Company

THEY WERE YOU.....................................Matt and Luisa

TRY TO REMEMBER (REPRISE)...................... El Gallo

ACT I

This play should be played on a platform. There is no scenery, but occasionally a stick may be held up to represent a wall. Or a cardboard moon may be hung upon a pole to indicate that it is night. When the audience enters the auditorium, the platform is clearly in sight, and there is a tattered drape across the front of it upon which is lettered THE FANTASTICKS.

During the OVERTURE, the members of the Company arrive and prepare to do the play. They take down the lettered drape, set out the Wooden Bench, and put the finishing touches on their costumes. When the MUSIC is over, they take their places and wait while the NARRATOR (EL GALLO) sings to the audience.

EL GALLO: Try to remember the kind of September
When life was slow and oh, so mellow.
Try to remember the kind of September
When grass was green and grain was yellow.
Try to remember the kind of September
When you were a tender and callow fellow.
Try to remember, and if you remember,
Then follow.

LUISA: Follow, follow, follow, follow, follow,
Follow, follow, follow, follow.

EL GALLO: Try to remember when life was so tender
That no one wept except the willow.
Try to remember when life was so tender
That dreams were kept beside your pillow.
Try to remember when life was so tender
That love was an ember about to billow.
Try to remember and if you remember,
Then follow.

LUISA: Follow, follow, follow, follow, follow,
Follow, follow, follow . . .

MATT: Follow, follow, follow, follow, follow,
Follow, follow, follow, follow.

FATHERS: Follow, follow, follow, follow, follow,
Follow, follow, follow, follow.

EL GALLO: Deep in December, it's nice to remember,

Although you know the snow will follow.
Deep in December, it's nice to remember:
Without a hurt the heart is hollow.
Deep in December, it's nice to remember
The fire of September that made us mellow.
Deep in December, our hearts should remember
And follow.

(Speaks to audience.)

Let me tell you a few things you may want to know
Before we begin the play.
First of all, the characters:
A Boy.
A Girl.
Two Fathers.
And — a Wall.

(MUTE comes forward, tips his hat.)

Anything else that's needed
We can get from out this box.

(EL GALLO and the MUTE quickly cross up to the large Trunk and remove the Prop Box, which they place on the stage floor.)

It's hard to know which is more important,
Or how it all began.
The Boy was born.
The Girl was born.
They grew up, quickly,
Went to school,
Became shy,
In their own ways and for different reasons.
Read Romances,
Studied cloud formations in the lazy afternoon,
And instead of reading textbooks,
Tried to memorize the moon.
And when the girl was fifteen —
(She was younger than the boy)
She began to notice something strange.
Her ugly duckling features
Had undergone a change.
In short, she was growing pretty.
For the first time in her whole life — pretty.

And the shock so stunned and thrilled her
That she became
Almost immediately
Incurably insane.
Observe:

(*MUSIC: LUISA steps off the platform and walks in a semicircle, in rhythm to the MUSIC. At the end of it, during the "button," the MUTE places the chair on the stage floor, so that LUISA may, on the final note, seat herself in it.*)

LUISA: The moon turns red on my birthday every year and it always will until somebody saves me and takes me back to my palace!

EL GALLO: That is a typical remark.
The other symptoms vary.
She thinks that she's a princess;
That her name must be in French,
Or sometimes Eurasian,
Although she isn't sure what that is.

LUISA: You see, no one can feel the way I feel
And have a father named Amos Babcock Bellomy.

(*On the platform, BELLOMY tips his hat and nods to the audience.*)

EL GALLO: She has a glue paste necklace
Which she thinks is really real.

(*EL GALLO nods to the MUTE, who quickly moves to the Prop Box, opens it, removes necklace, and hands it to LUISA.*)

LUISA: I found it in the attic
With my Mother's name inside.
It is my favorite possession.

EL GALLO: It's her fancy.

LUISA: It's my pride!

(*She has given him a reproachful look. EL GALLO nods and then steps back and sits on the Trunk, indicating that the stage is hers.*)

This morning a bird woke me up.

(*MUSIC.*)

It was a lark or a peacock
Or something like that.
Some strange sort of bird that I'd never heard.
And I said "hello"
And it vanished: flew away.
The very minute that I said "hello."
It was mysterious.

So do you know what I did?
I went over to my mirror
And brushed my hair two hundred times without
    stopping.
And as I was brushing it,
My hair turned mauve.

No, honestly! Mauve!
And then red.
And then sort of a deep blue when the sun hit it.

I'm sixteen years old,
And everyday something happens to me.
I don't know what to make of it.
When I get up in the morning to get dressed,
I can tell:
Something's different.
I like to touch my eyelids
Because they're never quite the same.

Oh! Oh! Oh!

(*MUSIC begins "under" and continues to build in speed
and volume as she clasps her arms around herself and
pours forth a torrent of pent-up passion.*)

I hug myself till my arms turn blue,
Then I close my eyes and I cry and cry
Till the tears come down
And I taste them. Ah!
I love to taste my tears!
I am special!
I am special!

(*Suddenly she clasps her hands in a fervent and heartfelt
prayer as the MUSIC stops.*)

Please, God, please!

Don't — let — me — be — normal!

(*And, rapturously, she sings.*)

I'd like to swim in a clear blue stream
Where the water is icy cold.
Then go to town
In a golden gown,
And have my fortune told.
Just once,
Just once,
Just once before I'm old.

I'd like to be — not evil,
But a little worldly wise.
To be the kind of girl designed
To be kissed upon the eyes.

I'd like to dance till two o'clock,
Or sometimes dance till dawn,
Or if the band could stand it,
Just go on and on and on!
Just once,
Just once,
Before the chance is gone!

I'd like to waste a week or two
And never do a chore.
To wear my hair unfastened
So it billows to the floor.

To —
Do the things I've dreamed about
But never done before!
Perhaps I'm bad, or wild, or mad,
With lots of grief in store,
But I want much more than keeping house!
Much more!
Much more!
Much more!

EL GALLO: Good.
And now the boy.
His story may be a wee bit briefer,
Because it's pretty much the same.

(*MUSIC: MATT rises and takes his place as the MUTE*

gets a Biology book and tosses it to him on the last note of the MUSIC.)

MATT: There is this girl.

EL GALLO: That is the essence.

MATT: There is this girl.

EL GALLO: I warn you: it may be monotonous.

MATT: There is this girl.

(Since he gets no interruption from EL GALLO, he continues.)

I'm nearly twenty years old.
I've studied Biology.
I've had an education.
I've been inside a lab:
Dissected violets.
I know the way things are.

I'm grown-up, stable,
Willing to conform.
I'm beyond such foolish notions.
And yet — in spite of my knowledge —
There is this girl.

She makes me young again!
And foolish.
And with her I perform the impossible:
I defy Biology!
And achieve Ignorance!

(MUSIC as he tosses the book back to the MUTE.)

There are no other ears but hers to hear the explosion of my soul! There are no other eyes but hers to make me wise, and despite what they say of species, there is not one plant or animal or any growing thing that is made quite the same as she is. It's stupid, of course, I know it. And immensely un-dignified. But I do love her!

EL GALLO: Look!

(Snaps his fingers and points to MUTE.)

This is the wall their fathers built between their houses.

(Everyone moves into position as the MUTE stands upstage center on the platform and holds out a stick to represent the "Wall.")

MATT: They built it ages ago — last month — when I came home from school. Poor fools, they built it to keep us apart. Maybe she's there now. I hope so — I'll see . . . I don't know what to call her. She's too vibrant for a name. What shall I call her?

(MUSIC: A Bell Tone. Ah! He has just thought of the perfect name. And he sings it.)

Juliet?

LUISA: *(Sings.)*
Yes dear!

MATT: Helena?

LUISA: Yes, dear?

MATT: *(Speaks.)*
And Cassandra. And Cleopatra. And Beatrice. And also

(Sings.)

Guinevere?

LUISA: What, dear?

MATT: *(Speaks to audience.)*
I think she's there.

(He moves to the Bench and sits, facing front. Thus, LUISA and MATT are on either side of the Bench, each not seeing the other because of the "Wall" between them.)

Can you hear me?

LUISA: Barely.

MATT: I've been speaking of you.

LUISA: To whom?

MATT: To them.

(He points to audience and she smiles.)

I told them that if someone were to ask me to describe you I would be utterly and totally speechless, except to say perhaps that you are Polaris or the in-side of a leaf.

LUISA: Speak a little louder.

MATT: *(Suddenly stands and sings vigorously.)*
I love you!

(LUISA swoons.)

If I were in the desert deep in sand,
And the sun was burning like a hot pomegranate:
Walking through a nightmare in the heat of a
   summer day,
Until my mind was parch-ed!
Then you are water . . .
Cool, clear water . . .
A refreshing glass of water!

LUISA: *(Rising from the floor.)*
What, dear?

MATT: Water!

(And down she goes again.)

Love! You are love!
Better far than a metaphor
Can ever, ever be.
Love! You are love!
My mystery — of love!

If the world was like an iceberg,
And everything was frozen,
And tears turned into icicles in the eye!
And snow came pouring —
And sleet and ice —
Came stabbing like a knife!
Then you are heat!
A fire alive with heat!
A flame that thaws the iceberg with its heat!

LUISA: Repeat.

MATT: You are heat!

(She swoons, then revives immediately to join him in song.)

Love!

(I am love!)
You are love!
    (I am love!)
Better far than a metaphor
Can ever, ever be!

Love!
    (I am love!)
You are love!
    (I am love!)
My mystery —
    (His mystery —)
Of love!

(*During this held note, they both climb up upon the
Bench and grab each other by the hand.*)

You are Polaris,
The one trustworthy star.
You are!
    (I am!)
You are!
    (I am!)

You are September,
A special mystery
To me!
    (To he!)
To me!
    (To he!)

MATT: You are sunlight! Moonlight!
Mountains! Valleys!
The microscopic inside of a leaf!
My joy!

LUISA: Yes, I am his joy!

MATT: My grief!

LUISA: Yes, I am his grief!

MATT: My star!

LUISA: Yes, I am his star!

MATT: My leaf!

LUISA: Yes, I am his leaf!

MATT: Oh. Love —

LUISA: I am love.

MATT: You are love —

LUISA: I am love.

BOTH: Better far than a metaphor
Can ever ever be.

MATT: Love —

LUISA: I am love.

MATT: You are love —

LUISA: I am love.

MATT: My mystery.

LUISA: His mystery —

BOTH: Of love . . .

Love . . .

Love . . . !

LUISA: (*When the applause is over.*)
Matt!

MATT: Luisa!

LUISA: Shh. Be careful.
I thought I heard a sound.

MATT: But you're trembling!

LUISA: My father loves to spy.

MATT: I know; I know.
I had to climb out through a window.
My father locked my room.

LUISA: Oh God, be careful!
Suppose you were to fall!

MATT: It's on the ground floor.

LUISA: Oh.

MATT: Still, the window's very small.
I could get stuck.

LUISA: This is madness, isn't it?

MATT: Yes, it's absolutely mad!

LUISA: And also very wicked?

MATT: Yes.

LUISA: I'm glad.

MATT: My father would be furious if he knew.

LUISA: Listen! I have had a vision.

MATT: Of disaster?

LUISA: No. Of azaleas.

MATT: Azaleas . . . ?

LUISA: I dreamed I was picking azaleas
When all at once this Duke —
Oh, he was very old,
I'd say nearly forty —
But attractive,
And very evil.

MATT: I hate him!

LUISA: And he had a retinue of scoundrels,
And they were hiding behind the rhododendrons,
And then all at once,
As I picked an azalea —
He leapt out!

MATT: God. I hate him!

LUISA: In my vision, how I struggled.
Like —
Like —
The Rape of the Sabine Women!
I cried "help!"

MATT: And I was nearby!

LUISA: Yes. Yes! You come rushing to the rescue.
And, single-handed, you fight off all his men,
And win —

MATT: And then —

LUISA: Celebration!

MATT: Fireworks!

46

LUISA: Fiesta!

MATT: Laughter!

LUISA: Our fathers give in!

MATT: We live happily ever after!

LUISA: (*To the audience.*)
There's no reason in the world why it can't happen exactly like that.

(*HUCKLEBEE clears his throat.*)

Someone's coming!

MATT: It's my father.

LUISA: Kiss me!

(*They kiss as MUSIC begins and HUCKLEBEE comes in with pruning shears and prunes away at a massive imaginary plant.*)

HUCK: Too much moisture!

(*To audience.*)

There are a great many things I could tell you about myself. I was once in the Navy; that's where I learned Horticulture. Yes, I have been the world over. I've seen it all: mountain cactus, the century plant, Japanese Ivy. And exotic ports, where bogwort was sold in the open market! I'm a man of experience and there is one thing that I've learned: Too much moisture is worse than none at all. Prune a plant. Avoid water. And go easy on manure. Moderation. That's the moral. That's my son's foot.

MATT: Hello, Father.

HUCK: What are you doing up in that tree?

MATT: Writing verses.

HUCK: Curses.

MATT: How's that?

HUCK: I offer a father's curses to the kind of education that makes our children fools. I sent this boy to school — to college. And I hope you know what that costs.

Did he learn to dig a cesspool? No. He's up there now "writing verses." Why do I always find you standing beside that wall?

MATT: I'm waiting for it to fall.
Besides, I like it.
I like its lovely texture,
And its pretty little eyes.

HUCK: Walls don't have eyes!

MATT: Then what do you call —
This flower?

LUISA: Sweet God, he's clever!

HUCK: Son, you are an ass. There you stand every day, writing verses, while who knows what our neighbor is up to on the other side of that wall. He's a villain! I'll not have it! I'll strip down those branches where an enemy could climb! I'll lime that wall with bottles! I'll jag it up with glass!

LUISA: Ahh!

HUCK: What was that?

MATT: Some broken willow — some little wounded bird.

HUCK: Maybe. But walls have ears even though they don't have eyes. I'll just take a look.

(*Starts to climb, then stops.*)

Ahh! There's that stiffness again.

(*Confidentially, to the audience.*)

The result of my Navy career. Here, son. You climb. You can see for me.

MATT: All right, Father.

(*MUSIC as MATT leaps onto the Bench and smiles down at LUISA.*)

HUCK: What do you see?

MATT: (*Stage whisper, giving her the flower.*)
I love you.

LUISA: I love you, too.

(*Blows him a kiss.*)

HUCK: What are you mumbling about? Get down from there if there's nothing to be seen! Down I say!

MATT: I obey.

HUCK: You're an idiot. So I've decided you need to be married. So I went shopping this morning and picked you out a wife.

LUISA: Ahh!

HUCK: There's that sound again.

MATT: Anguished bird.

HUCK: Weeping willow?
It may be.
But let's get back to business:
Son, I've picked you out a girl. A pearl.

MATT: And if I prefer a diamond?

HUCK: How dare you prefer a diamond
When I've just offered you a pearl!

MATT: Listen carefully to what I have to say.
Listen, wall.
And flowers. And willow, too.
And wounded bird.
And Father, you
May as well listen, too.

(*HUCKLEBEE starts to speak, but MATT cuts him off.*)

I will not wed by your wisdom.
I will not walk neatly into a church
And contract out to prolongate my race.
I will not go wedding in a too-tight suit
Nor be witnessed when I take my bride.

HUCK: You will do —

MATT: No!

(*MUSIC as MATT gets more and more carried away.*)

I'll marry, when I marry,
In my own particular way;
And my bride shall dress in sunlight

With rain for her wedding veil.
Out in the open,
With no one standing by.
No song except September
Being sung in the busy grass!
No sound except our heartbeats —
Roaring!
Like a flower alive with bees!
Without benefit of neighbor!
Without benefit of book!
Except perhaps her handprint
As she presses her hand in mine!
Except perhaps her imprint
As she gives me her golden hair!
In a field, while kneeling,
Being joined by the joy of life!

There!
In the air!
In the open!
That's how I plan to wive!

HUCK: Son . . .
You need pruning.
Come inside and write "simplicity" two hundred times without stopping. Perhaps that will improve your style.

(MUSIC as MATT and HUCKLEBEE cross upstage and sit on the platform, their backs to the audience. Meanwhile, BELLOMY stands up, watering can in hand, and comes downstage, pantomiming watering the plants in his garden.)

BELL: That's right, drink away. Open up your thirsty little mouths.

(To the audience.)

I'm her father. And believe me, it isn't easy. Perhaps that's why I love vegetables. So dependable. I mean, you plant a radish, and you know what you're about. You don't get a turnip or a cabbage, no. Plant a turnip, get a turnip; plant a cabbage, get a cabbage. While with children — I thought I had planted a turnip or at worst perhaps an avocado: something remotely useful. I'm a merchant. I sell buttons. What need do I have for a rose? — There she is. Missy, you must go inside.

LUISA: I've told you; I'm a princess.

BELL: You're a button-maker's daughter. Now, go inside as you're told. Our enemy is beyond that wall. Up to something: I can feel it!

(*Shouts over the "Wall."*)

Him and his no-good son!

(*LUISA angrily steps off the platform.*)

Look out, you've stepped in my peppers! That settles it. I'll put a fence here by this wall. A high fence, with barbed stickers! An arsenal of wire!

LUISA: A fence is expensive, Papa.

BELL: Expensive? Well, I'll build it myself. Go inside — Do as I tell you!

(*LUISA crosses up and sits on the platform, her back to the audience.*)

Is she gone? — Ah, yes, she's gone.

(*Quickly he moves to the stage right pole and, holding on with one hand, he cups his other hand to his mouth and yodels.*)

Oh, lady le di le da loo . . .

(*As BELLOMY listens for a reply, HUCKLEBEE quickly rises and crosses to the stage left pole, where he takes the same stance and echoes the same yodel.*)

HUCK: Oh, lady le di le da loo. . .

(*MUSIC as they scramble up the bench and noisily embrace over the "Wall."*)

BELL: Hucklebee!

HUCK: Bellomy!

BELL: Neighbor!

HUCK: Friend!

BELL: How's the gout?

HUCK: I barely notice. And your asthma?

BELL: A trifle.

        (*Coughs.*)

        I endure it.

HUCK: Well, it's nearly settled.

BELL: (*Hasn't a clue.*)
        What is?

HUCK: The marriage! They're nearly ready. I hid in the bushes to listen. Oh, it's something! They're out of their minds with love!

BELL: Hurray!

HUCK: (*To audience.*)
        My son — he is fantastic!

BELL: (*To audience.*)
        My daughter is fantastic, too.
        They're both of them mad.

HUCK: They are geese!

BELL: It was a clever plan we had:
        To build this wall.

HUCK: Yes. And to pretend to feud.

BELL: Just think if they knew
        That we wanted them wed.

HUCK: A prearranged marriage —

BELL: They'd rather be dead!

HUCK: Children!

BELL: Lovers!

HUCK: Fantasticks!

BELL: Geese!

HUCK: How clever we are.

BELL: How crafty to know.

HUCK: To manipulate children

BELL: You merely say —

BOTH: No...

(*Sing.*)

Ohhhhhhhhhh!

Dog's got to bark, a mule's got to bray.
Soldiers must fight and preachers must pray.
And children, I guess, must get their own way
The minute that you say no.

Why did the kids pour jam on the cat?
Raspberry jam all over the cat?
Why should the kids do something like that,
When all that we said was no?

HUCK: My son was once afraid to swim.
The water made him wince.
Until I said he mustn't swim:
S'been swimmin' ever since!

BOTH: S'been swimmin' ever since!

Ohhhhhhhhhh!

Dog's got to bark, a mule's got to bray.
Soldiers must fight and preachers must pray.
And children, I guess, must get their own way
The minute that you say no.

Why did the kids put beans in their ears?
No one can hear with beans in their ears.
After a while the reason appears.
They did it cause we said no.

BELL: Your daughter brings a young man in,
Says "Do you like him, Pa?"
Just tell her he's a fool and then:
You've got a son-in-law!

BOTH: You've got a son-in-law!

Ohhhhhh —

Sure as a June comes right after May!
Sure as the night comes right after day!
You can be sure the devil's to pay
The minute that you say no.

Make sure you never say
No!

BELL: *(When the song is over.)*
But there's one problem left.

HUCK: How to end the feud?

BELL: Exactly, you guessed it.
We mustn't let them know.

HUCK: Oh, no, if they knew —
We're finished.

BELL: We're through.

HUCK: I think I've found the answer.
It's delicious. Very theatrical.

BELL: Tell me.

HUCK: An ab-duc-tion!

BELL: Who's ab-duc-ted?

HUCK: Your daughter.

BELL: Who abducts her?

HUCK: A professional abductor.
I've hired the very man!

(MUSIC as EL GALLO enters with a flourish.)

EL GALLO: Gentlemen, good evening.

BELL: What the devil?

HUCK: Who are you?

EL GALLO: I was sent for.
A maiden in distress.

HUCK: Oh, yes, of course, you are the famous El Gallo.

(He pronounces it American, like the wine.)

EL GALLO: *(Pronounces it Spanish, like the bullfighter.)*
El Gayo!

(And, quick as lightning, EL GALLO flicks his red scarf from out of his shirt, causing both FATHERS to start nervously.)

HUCK: Oh — si, si.

EL GALLO: Si.

HUCK: (*To BELLOMY.*)
See. This is what I was about to tell you. We hire this man to assist us. He starts to kidnap your daughter. My son runs in to save her. Then, a battle.

                 (*HUCKLEBEE and EL GALLO look at BELLOMY, who shows no signs of comprehension.*)

EL GALLO: I allow the boy to defeat me.

HUCK: My son becomes a hero ... And the feud is over forever.

BELL: (*He finally gets it.*)
Oooh!

                 (*Then, craftily, to EL GALLO.*)

                 How much for such a drama?

EL GALLO: That, Señor, depends.

BELL: On what?

EL GALLO: What else? The quality of the "rape."

BELL: No.

                 (*He starts to leave, but EL GALLO intercepts him.*)

EL GALLO: Forgive me. The attempted "rape." The abduction. The seizure. The kidnapping. Call it what you will. To plunder. To pillage. To carry off by force. From the Latin "rapere," meaning "to seize." You've heard, of course, of *The Rape of Lucrece*.

HUCK: Of course.

EL GALLO: *The Rape of the Lock?*

HUCK: Absolutely. Absolutely! — I heard her speak of Sabine Women.

BELL: Well, it doesn't sound right to me.

EL GALLO: It is, though, I assure you.
As a matter of fact, it's standard.

                 (*Acts it out.*)

                 The lovers meet in secret. And so forth.
A group of villains interrupts them. And so forth.
The boy fights off pirates, Indians, bandits.

The parents relent. Happy ending. And so forth.
All of it quite standard.

BELL: What about the cost? And so forth.

EL GALLO: Cost goes by type.
In your case, I think I would recommend
a "First Class!"

BELL: You mean, we get a choice?

EL GALLO: Yes, of course. With regular union rates.

(*Sings as he leaps onto platform and strikes a Flamenco pose.*)

Rape!
R-a-a-a-pe!
Raa-aa-aa-pe!

A pretty rape.
A literary rape!

We've the obvious open schoolboy rape,
With little mandolins and perhaps a cape.
The rape by coach; it's little in request.
The rape by day, but the rape by night is best.

Just try to see it.
And you will soon agree, señors,
Why —
Invite regret,
When you can get the sort of rape
You'll never ever forget!

You can get the rape emphatic.
You can get the rape polite.
You can get the rape with Indians:
A truly charming sight.
You can get the rape on horseback;
They all say it's new and gay.
So you see the sort of rape
Depends on what you pay.
It depends on what you
Pay.

HUCK: (*To BELLOMY.*)
The kids will love it.
It depends on what you

BELL: Pay!

HUCK: So why be stingy?
It depends on what you —

EL GALLO: The spectacular rape,
With costumes ordered from the East.
Requires rehearsal
And takes a dozen men at least.
A couple of singers,
And a string quartet.
A major production.
Requires a set.

BELL: Sounds expensive.

EL GALLO: Just try to see it,
And you will soon si, si señors,
Why —
Invite regret,
When you can get the sort of rape
You'll never ever forget!

You can get the rape emphatic.
You can get the rape polite.
You can get the rape with Indians:
A truly charming sight.
You can get the rape on horseback;
They all say it's distingué.
So you see the sort of rape
Depends on what you pay.

EL GALLO
& HUCK: So you see the sort of rape
Depends on what you pay.

EL GALLO: It depends on what you pay.

HUCK: So why be stingy
It depends on what you
Pay.

BELL: Pay! Pay! Pay!

HUCK: The kids will love it.
It depends on what you —

EL GALLO: The comic rape.
Perhaps it's just a trifle too unique.

Romantic rape:
Done while canoeing on a moonlit creek.

BELL: That's kind of pretty.

EL GALLO: The gothic rape!
I play "Valkyrie" on a bass bassoon!
The drunken rape.
It's done completely in a cheap saloon.

BELL: Nothing cheap!

EL GALLO: The rape Venetian —
Needs a blue lagoon.
The rape with moonlight
Or without a moon.
Moonlight is expensive but it's in demand.
A military rape!
It's done with drummers and a band.
You understand?

HUCK: I understand.

EL GALLO: It's very grand.

BELL: It's very grand.

EL GALLO: It's done with drums and a great big brass band!
Yeah!

(*EL GALLO and the FATHERS dance.*)

BELL: It's so Spanish. That's why I like it!

HUCK: I like it, too. Ai, yi, yi.

(*At the end of the dance, EL GALLO strikes a Flamenco-like pose on the platform and sings.*)

EL GALLO: Just try to see it!

BELL: I see it!

HUCK: I see it!

EL GALLO: And you will soon si, si señors,

ALL THREE: Why —
Invite regret
When you can get the sort of rape
You'll never ever forget!

(EL GALLO leaps up onto the Bench and strikes an opera-type pose, with hands clasped, as he sings in over-dramatic fashion: "Oh, rape! Sweet rape!" etc.)

FATHERS: We can get the rape emphatic.
We can get the rape polite.
We can get the rape with Indians:
A truly charming sight.
We can get the rape on horseback;
They all say it is new and gay.

ALL THREE: So you see the sort of rape
Depends on what you pay.

So you see the sort of rape
Depends on what you pay.

So you see the sort of rape
Depends on what you pay.

Depends a lot on what you —

(Suddenly MUSIC stops as HUCKLEBEE excitedly grabs BELLOMY by the arm and says:)

HUCK: I say they're only young once. Let's order us a "First Class!"

ALL THREE: *(Sing.)*
Ra — aa — aa — pe!
Olé!

EL GALLO: *(When the number is over.)*
One Rape, "First Class."

BELL: With trimmings!

EL GALLO: With trimmings. Now, let's see — is it to be a big affair, or intimate?

BELL: We thought — just the children.

EL GALLO: I mean afterwards, at the party.

BELL: No. Just the immediate family.

EL GALLO: No guests? Perhaps a gathering on the lawn?

BELL: Too expensive. Just the immediate family will be enough.

EL GALLO: As you wish. That means the orchestra can go

home. Still, big affairs are nice.

HUCK: Perhaps some other time.

EL GALLO: All right then. You'd better go home and rehearse your parts.

(*MUSIC. The FATHERS sing as they hurry back to their places.*)

FATHERS: We can get the rape emphatic.
We can get the rape polite.
We can get the rape with Indians:
A truly charming sight.
We can get the rape on horseback;
They all say it's new and gay.
So you see the sort of rape depends on what you pay.
It depends on what you pay.
Olé!

EL GALLO: La. Time is rushing. And a major production to do. I need actors — extra actors — to stage my elaborate Rape. But I'm not worried. Something will turn up. I can sense it in the air.

(*DRUMBEAT is heard from deep inside the Trunk.*)

There — you hear? What did I tell you?

(*The MUTE opens the Trunk and MORTIMER emerges dressed in a loin cloth and a feather, and playing a drum. He is followed at once by HENRY, an ancient actor down on his luck.*)

HENRY: (*Climbs out of the Trunk, crosses to the center and strikes a pose on the Prop Box after being helped onto it by MORTIMER.*)
Sir, the Players have arrived!

(*He throws into the air a small handful of confetti, which unfortunately comes falling down onto his face.*)

EL GALLO: Señor, the Players are most welcome.

HENRY: Don't look at us like we are, sir. Please. Remove ten pounds of road dust from these ag-ed wrinkled cheeks. See make-up, caked, in glowing powder pink! Imagine a beard, full blown and blowing, like the whiskers of a bear! And hair! Imagine hair. In a box I've got all colors, so I beg you — imagine hair! And not these clothes. Oh no, no, no. Dear God, not rags like any beggar has. But see me in a doublet! Mortimer, fetch the doublet.

(*MORTIMER sheathes him in a worn out doublet which he has hurriedly retrieved from the Trunk.*)

There — Imagine! It's torn; I know — forget it. It vanishes under light. That's it! That's the whole trick; try to see me under light! I recite! Say a cue. You'll see. I'll know it. Go on. Say one. Try me.

EL GALLO: "Friends, Romans, Countrymen."

HENRY: It's what?

EL GALLO: "Friends, Romans, Countrymen."

HENRY: — Don't tell me, I can get it. Let's see. "Friends, Romans? Countrymen."

(*MORTIMER whispers it to him.*)

Why yes! Of course! That's easy. Why didn't you pick something hard?

(*Steps onto the Bench with MORTIMER's help and strikes a suitably dramatic pose.*)

Watch this.

"Friends, Romans, Countrymen —
Screw your courage to the sticking place!
And be not sick and pale with grief
That thou — her handmaidens —
Should be far more fair
Than she . . .
Is . . . "

How's that?

EL GALLO: Amazing!

HENRY: Try to see it under light! I assure you — it's dazzling! I'm Henry Albertson. Perhaps you recall my Hamlet?

EL GALLO: Of course.

HENRY: (*Stunned.*)
You remember? Would you like to see the clippings?

EL GALLO: Perhaps later.

HENRY: As you wish. I preserve them. Who knows — I may write a book someday.

(*MORTIMER laughs. Seeing that no one else is amused, especially HENRY, he abruptly cuts short his laughter.*)

This is Mortimer. He does death scenes. He's been with me for forty years. He's an expert. Want to see one?

(*EL GALLO hesitates and then nods "yes."*)

Go ahead, Mortimer. Die for the man.

(*MORTIMER, rather shyly, steps to center and "takes the stage." First he pantomimes seeing something in the distance. Then, also in pantomime, he gets his bow and places an arrow in it. Drawing the string of the bow to its full potential, the very "pull" begins to turn the whole thing around. To his amazement and horror, MORTI-MER watches as the arrow comes slowly around to point at his own stomach. Then, with a sudden movement, the arrow fires into his mid-section and he falls forward — hoist, as they say, upon his own petard.*)

HENRY: You see! What did I tell you! Now, down to business! You, sir, need players?

EL GALLO: For a love scene. Have you done romantic drama, Henry?

HENRY: That, sir, is my speciality. Have you never seen my . . .

(*Creaks down to one knee.*)

Romeo?

EL GALLO: I'm afraid not.

HENRY: Oh well, I have the clippings.

(*Starts to get them, but EL GALLO grabs him.*)

EL GALLO: Henry, here's the path!

HENRY: (*In the "scene" already.*)
Ah ha!

EL GALLO: We'll have these players play something like the abduction of the maiden before this lover!

HENRY: And if he but blench!

EL GALLO: We'll stand our ground!
And fight until the lot of us is downed!

HENRY: Nobly done!

EL GALLO: This way, Henry.

HENRY: Young man.

(*EL GALLO, who has moved to the side, turns back. HENRY indicates by a gesture that he needs help, so EL GALLO returns and helps him down from the Bench.*)

Thank you.

(*HENRY starts to exit, when suddenly there is heard:*)

MORT: Psst. Psst.
'Enry.

HENRY: (*Trying to locate who it is through his myopic eyes.*)
Hmm?

MORT: (*Speaks with a thick Cockney accent.*)
Where do you want me?

HENRY: Oh! Off Left, Mortimer. Off Left.

(*To audience.*)

Indians are always Off Left!

MORT: 'Enry

HENRY: Hmm?

MORT: Wot's me cue?

HENRY: I'll tell you when it's time.

MORT: Righto.

(*Starts off.*)

HENRY: Oh. And Mortimer. Don't forget: dress the stage, dress the stage! Dear friend, don't cluster up when you die!

(*MORTIMER, willing but confused, nods in agreement and exits left, bumping into scenery on the way.*)

HENRY: *(Speaking to audience.)*
He's not really an Indian, you know.

(To EL GALLO.)

Well, that about does it, I think. I imagine we'd better hide.

EL GALLO: Oh.

(Snaps his fingers and MUTE goes to the Prop Box and removes the wooden Moon which he holds up in the air.)

I nearly forgot. I promised them moonlight.

(MUSIC: A HARP glissando as EL GALLO takes the Moon and hangs it on one of the poles. The lights become romantic and soft as the MUTE takes a delicately tattered blue and green china-silk "Glen Drop" and hangs it between the two upstage poles on the platform.)

HENRY: *(Looking up at the blue lights, touched.)*
Amazing!

EL GALLO: Beautiful, eh? A lover's moon. You go ahead, Henry. I'll be right there.

(As HENRY exits, EL GALLO takes his place on the platform and speaks to the audience.)

You wonder how these things begin.
Well, this begins with a glen.
It begins with a season which,
For want of a better word,
We might as well call — September.

(As MUSIC begins "under.")

It begins with a forest where the woodchucks woo,
And leaves wax green,
And vines entwine like lovers; try to see it.
Not with your eyes, for they are wise,
But see it with your ears:
The cool green breathing of the leaves.
And hear it with the inside of your hand:
The soundless sound of shadows flicking light.
Celebrate sensation.
Recall that secret place.
You've been there, you remember:
That special place where once —

64

Just once — in your crowded sunlit lifetime,
You hid away in shadows from the tyranny of time.
That spot beside the clover
Where someone's hand held your hand
And love was sweeter than the berries,
Or the honey,
Or the stinging taste of mint.

It is September —
Before a rainfall —
A perfect time to be in love.

(*MATT and LUISA have risen and now come forward into the moonlight.*)

MATT: Hello.

LUISA: Hello.
My father is going to be very angry.

MATT: I know. So is mine.

LUISA: We've never been here at night.

MATT: No.

LUISA: It's different from the day.

MATT: Are you frightened?

LUISA: Yes. — No.

(*She looks at him.*)

It's cold here. There's going to be a storm.

MATT: (*Indicating his sweater.*)
Would you like my jacket?

LUISA: No, thank you. Matt.

MATT: Yes?

LUISA: My hand is trembling.

MATT: Don't be afraid. Please.

LUISA: All right. I promise.

(*EL GALLO signals for thunder. MUSIC. LUISA rushes into MATT's arms as the MUTE throws some paper "leaves" into the air. Then EL GALLO and the MUTE retire to the side and watch.*)

MATT: There, there. It's all right.

LUISA: Matt, take care of me. Teach me. I don't want to be awkward — or afraid. I love you, Matt. I want there to be a happy ending.

MATT: I promise that there will be.

(*Holds out his hand.*)

Look.

LUISA: What?

MATT: My hand is trembling, too.

LUISA: (*Sings.*)
Hear how the wind begins to whisper.
See how the leaves go streaming by.
Smell how the velvet rain is falling,
Out where the fields are warm and dry.
Now is the time to run inside and stay.
Now is the time to find a hideaway —
Where we can stay.

(*Both of them sit on the Prop Box as the MUTE appears above and behind the Glen Drop, observing.*)

MATT: (*Sings.*)
Soon it is gonna rain.
I can see it.
Soon it's gonna rain.
I can tell.
Soon it's gonna rain.
What are we gonna do?

Soon it's gonna rain.
I can feel it.
Soon it's gonna rain.
I can tell.
Soon it's gonna rain.
What'll we do with you?

(*MUTE holds out small tree branches as MATT and LUISA move up to the platform and sit on the Bench.*)

We'll find four limbs of a tree.
We'll build four walls and a floor.
We'll bind it over with leaves,

And duck inside to stay.

(*MUTE begins to sprinkle them with confetti "rain."*)

BOTH: Then we'll let it rain.
We'll not feel it.
Then we'll let it rain,
Rain pell-mell.

And we'll not complain
If it never stops at all.
We'll live and love
Within our own four walls.

MATT: (*As MUSIC continues.*)
Would you like for me to show you around the castle?

LUISA: Oh. Yes, please.

(*And they begin to dance — at first grand and sweeping and then more and more tenderly as the wind continues to swirl in. As the "thunder" rolls, MATT sings.*)

MATT: We'll find four limbs of a tree.
We'll build four walls and a floor.
We'll bind it over with leaves,
And run inside to stay.

LUISA: Soon it's gonna rain!

MATT: Come run inside to stay!

LUISA: Soon it's gonna rain!

MATT: For soon it's gonna rain.
I can see it.
I can feel it.
Run inside and —

(*And now she rushes into his arms, and as they sit on the Bench the MUTE, standing above and behind the drape, sprinkles them with paper "rain."*)

BOTH: Then we'll let it rain.
We'll not feel it.
Then we'll let it rain.
Rain pell-mell.

MATT: And we'll not complain

LUISA: Happy ending!

MATT: If it never stops at all.

LUISA: Then we'll let it rain.
Why complain?

BOTH: We'll live and love within our walls.
Happily we'll live and love,
No cares at all.
Happily we'll live and love
Within our castle walls.

(*At the end of the number, during the applause, HENRY emerges from the side, wearing a short, tattered black cape.*)

HENRY: (*Accepting the applause as his own.*)
Thank you. Thank you.

(*Signals to MUSICIANS.*)

Orchestra! Accelerando con molto!

(*As the MUSIC begins for the Rape Ballet, HENRY calls out "Swords" to the MUTE, who rushes to the Prop Box and removes four wooden sticks.*)

Indians, ready? Indians — Rape!

(*And MORTIMER springs out of his hiding place, also in a short, black cape. He snatches up the astonished LUISA right before the eyes of the equally astonished MATT and starts to carry her out. But HENRY, in a fury, interrupts him.*)

No, no. Off Left, damn it!

MORT: All right. All right.

(*And he faithfully totes her towards stage left. But now MATT has recovered himself sufficiently to intercept them. He struggles with MORTIMER as HENRY grabs up the disentangled LUISA. MORTIMER and HENRY pick up the girl and try to carry her out. The MUTE hands MATT the drum sticks to MORTI-MER's Indian Drum, and MATT floors both the old actors with a mighty whop of the sticks. LUISA rushes up to her protector as HENRY struggles to his feet.*)

HENRY: (*Feeling his head.*)
A touch, a touch. I do confess it.

(*Now, the moment is ripe for the big scene. HENRY rushes to the side and yells out: "Ready? Cavalry!" Which is the cue for EL GALLO to enter into the fray. EL GALLO sweeps on with a flourish, wearing a beautiful, full black cape with a red lining. The MUTE supplies both him and MATT with wooden swords and they begin to fight. During the midst of their battle, EL GALLO is thrown to the side and HENRY catches him and yells out:*)

Once more, dear friends, into the breach!

(*At this signal the MUTE supplies HENRY and MORTIMER with stick swords and all three "villains" swordfight our young hero at once, not at all unlike the Douglas Fairbanks movies of the good old days. They advance. They retreat. Then — with a mighty push, MATT sends them all sprawling to the floor. MORTIMER, risen, rushes forward — is killed dramatically. HENRY rises — and as he charges, cries out:*)

God for Harry, England, and Saint Geo . . . ough!

(*The last word becomes a vivid "ouch" as he is wounded and falls dead. Only EL GALLO is left now. He and MATT square off and have at it. For a while it's nip and tuck as the two men fight up and down the Prop Box, and upon the platform, and clash together every once in a while so that they stand gritting, tooth to tooth, across the crisscrossed "sabers." In the end, EL GALLO allows himself to be stabbed in the stomach — and he dies in so grand a manner that MORTIMER cannot resist a look of admiration. EL GALLO dies like a diva in the opera, rising again and again from the floor to give one last dramatic, agonized twitch.*)

(*After the Ballet, when EL GALLO has gone down for the last time, the MUSIC becomes jolly and triumphant. The young lovers rush upon the little platform and embrace in a pretty tableau. The FATHERS rush in, too. And embrace, too. And get upon the platform to finish off the "Living Statues" type of tableau.*)

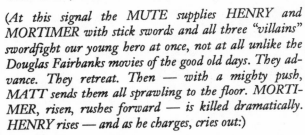

LUISA: Matt!

MATT: Luisa!

HUCK: Son!

BELL: Daughter!

HUCK: (*To BELLOMY.*)
Neighbor!

BELL: (*To HUCKLEBEE.*)
Friend!

LUISA: (*To the world.*)
I always knew there would be a happy ending!

   (*The MUSIC suddenly stops. They all freeze as EL GALLO rises, rather painfully, from the dead.*)

EL GALLO: (*Feeling his back.*)
I think I pulled something.

MORT: (*Gathering up the wood swords.*)
Oh, you get a bit sore at first, dying like that. It's not the easiest 'fing in the business. But I like it. I've been dying for forty years. Ever since I was a boy. Ah, you should have seen me in those days. I could die off a twenty foot cliff — backwards! People used to cry out: "Die again, Mortimer — die again!" But of course I never did.

   (*And now MORTIMER returns swords to MUTE and hurries over to help HENRY rise from the dead.*)

EL GALLO: Well, Henry. Are you off now?

HENRY: (*Taking Moon off pole.*)
Yes. Going somewhere. There's not much left to the old company anymore. Just Mortimer and me. But we make out. I recite Shakespeare. And Mortimer dies. There's usually an audience — somewhere.

   (*Starts to go.*)

EL GALLO: Henry.

HENRY: Mmm?

   (*EL GALLO points.*)

Oh. I nearly forgot. Here's your moon.

EL GALLO: Thank you. "Good night, Sweet Prince."

(*HENRY turns to him, enthralled. He strikes a pose upon the platform, but as he starts to declaim, a Spotlight comes up on MORTIMER.*)

HENRY: "And flights of angels sing thee . . .

(*He stops. Looks at MORTIMER. Looks at Light. Then, cupping his hands to his mouth, he shouts out to the Light Crew.*)

That's my light!

(*Light goes out on MORTIMER and comes up on HENRY.*)

Thank you.

(*Resumes pose.*)

"And flights of angels sing thee to thy rest. Why doth the drum come hither?"

(*Thinking this is a cue, MORTIMER steps forward and hits his drum with all his strength, causing HENRY to almost expire of cardiac arrest. Seeing he has "goofed" again, MORTIMER steps upstage and lowers his head so that HENRY may pluck out his one Indian feather.*)

Remember, Mortimer, there are no small actors. Only small parts.

(*HENRY and MORTIMER have stepped back into the Trunk, and just before he disappears under the lid which the MUTE is closing, HENRY looks out to the audience and speaks.*)

Remember me — in light!

(*And he is gone. EL GALLO looks at the LOVERS and their PARENTS still "frozen" on the platform. Like a choral conductor, he conducts them in a short contrapuntal selection called "Happy Ending" as they break from the freeze and begin to assemble the tableau with much posing and embracing and shaking of hands.*)

FATHERS: Ha, ha, ha, ha. — Ha, ha, ha, ha. Etc.

LUISA: Ha — ha, ha, ha, ha. Ha, ha, ha.
Ha — ha, ha, ha, ha. — Ha, ha, ha. Etc.

MATT: Love,
    You are love.
    Better far than a metaphor
    Can ever, ever be!
    Love.
    You are love.
    My mystery —
    Of love.
    Love, love, love, love!

ALL: Love! Love! Love!

(And the FATHERS and the CHILDREN "freeze" into place in an intricate tableau.)

EL GALLO: *(When they are through singing.)*
    Very pretty, eh?
    Worthy of Watteau.
    A group of living statues.
    What do they call it? A tableau.

    Hmmmmm.
    I wonder if they can hold it.
    They'll try to, I suppose.
    And yet it won't be easy
    To hold such a pretty pose.

    We'll see.
    We'll leave them for a little.
    Then we'll see.

(EL GALLO and the MUTE hang the FANTAS-TICKS drape in front of the actors. EL GALLO starts to leave, but the MUTE taps him on the shoulder and EL GALLO, remembering, smiles and says to the audience:)

Act One is over.
It's the Intermission now.

ACT II

MUSIC as EL GALLO enters, carrying the Moon. He nods to the MUTE, who undoes the rope and removes the FANTASTICKS drape on the little platform stage. The PARENTS and the LOVERS are still there, poised in their pretty tableau. But they seem less graceful now, as if there were some pain involved in holding the pose so long.

EL GALLO: Their moon was cardboard, fragile.
It was very apt to fray,
And what was last night scenic
May seem cynic by today.
The play's not done.
Oh, no — not quite,
For life never ends in the moonlit night;
And despite what pretty poets say,
The night is only half the day.

So we would like to truly finish
What was foolishly begun.
For the story is not ended
And the play is never done
Until we've all of us been burned a bit
And burnished by — the sun!

(He reverses the Moon. On the other side is the Sun. The MUSIC changes — grows more intense as EL GALLO hangs the Sun on one of the poles and then sits on the Trunk to watch. And one by one, the PARENTS and the CHILDREN begin to break the perfect image of the tableau. Their eyes sting in the red hot sun. The MUSIC underneath is sour, disgruntled.)

HUCK: It's hot.

BELL: What?

HUCK: Hot!

BELL: Oh. Ssssssss.

(MUSIC, as they all try unsuccessfully to regain the pose.)

LUISA: And now we can meet in the sunlight.

MATT: And now there is no more wall.

LUISA: Aren't we happy?

MATT: Yes. Aren't we?

(*MUSIC: a sour CHORD.*)

LUISA: (*Speaking to audience.*)
He looks different in the sunlight.

MATT: (*To audience.*)
I'm not ready to get married yet.

LUISA: I thought he was taller, somehow.

MATT: When you get right down to it, she's only the girl next door.

(*CHORD.*)

HUCK: Neighbor.

BELL: Friend.

HUCK: In-law.

BELL: Ugh.

(*CHORD.*)

HUCK: This is what we've always wanted.
Our gardens are one.

BELL: We're merged.

HUCK: Related.

BELL: Amalga-

HUCK: Mated.

BELL: Well . . . .

(*HUCKLEBEE gets his clippers and BELLOMY his watering can.*)

LUISA: What shall we do today?

MATT: Whatever you say.

LUISA: And tomorrow?

MATT: The same!

(*CHORD.*)

I wonder where that road goes.

LUISA: I'd like to take my hair down and go swimming in a stream.

(CHORD.)

HUCK: Water, Water, Water!

BELL: What did you say?

HUCK: I said, Water, Water, Water!

BELL: Clip, Clip, Clip!

HUCK: What?

BELL: You're clipping my kumquat!

HUCK: Rot!

(MUSIC begins "under.")

LUISA: This plum is too ripe!

MATT: Sorry.
Please don't watch me while I'm eating.

LUISA: Sorry!

HUCK: You're about to drown that magnolia!

BELL: Sorry!
You're — standing — in — my — KUMQUAT!

HUCK: Sorry!

(And the MUSIC for the quartet begins, first as solos, and then as a round, as each of them takes his turn pacing around the stage.)

LUISA: Take away the golden moonbeam.
Take away the tinsel sky.
What at night seems oh so scenic
May be cynic by and by.

MATT: Take away the painted sunset.
Take away the blue lagoon.
What at night seems oh so scenic
May be cynic much too soon.

HUCK: Take away the sense of drama.
Take away the puppet play.
What at night seems oh so scenic
May be cynic by today.

BELL: Take away the secret meetings.
Take away the chance to fight.
What at night seems oh so scenic
May be cynic in the light.

ALL: So take it away and paint it up right!
So take it away and decorate it!
So take it away; that sun is too bright!

LUISA: I say that it really is a pity.

LUISA
& MATT: It used to be so pretty.

(*And now they begin the round, snapping their fingers vigorously as they each of them joins in. All are facing front in a very presentational manner. Each of them drops out at a certain point of the round, and they stop snapping their fingers when they do.*)

LUISA: Take away the golden moonbeam.
Take away the tinsel sky.
What at night seems oh so scenic
May be cynic by and by.

MATT: (*Beginning with LUISA's second line.*)
Take away the painted sunset.
Take away the blue lagoon.
What at night seems oh so scenic
May be cynic much too soon.

HUCK: (*Beginning with MATT's second line.*)
Take away the sense of drama.
Take away the puppet play.
What at night seems oh so scenic
May be cynic by today.

BELL: (*Beginning with HUCKLEBEE's second line.*)
Take away the secret meetings.
Take away the chance to fight.
What at night seems oh so scenic
May be cynic in the light.

HUCK &
BELL: By today,

HUCK,
BELL &
MATT: Much too soon.

ALL: By and by.

MATT: (*Speaks.*)
This plum is too ripe!

(*Tosses plum to MUTE.*)

HUCK,
BELL &
LUISA: Sorry!

MATT: (*As soon as the MUSIC is over.*)
I miss the moon.

LUISA: So do I.

HUCK: I was a fool to tear down that wall.

BELL: So was I. I hate people tromping in my garden!

HUCK: What do you mean, your garden? I want you to
know —

BELL: (*Simultaneously.*)
Mine! That's what I mean — mine! This is —

LUISA: Please. No fighting.
You see, I come like Cassandra
With a figleaf in my hand.

BELL: It was Minerva.

HUCK: And that's a plum.

LUISA: Well!

MATT: Don't mind them, dear.
I think they're jealous.

HUCK: Jealous?

MATT: Of us. Of our passion — and our youth.

BELL: Fantastic!

MATT: You see — they are jealous!

LUISA: It's sweet — just like drama.
Fathers always play the fool.

(*Both giggle knowingly.*)

HUCK: I could speak, if I chose to —

MATT: Speak what?

BELL: Shh. Better not.

HUCK: No. I'll be silent.

(*To MATT.*)

But you'd better not push it much further.

MATT: You forget that I'm a hero.
After all, there's my rapier.

LUISA: And my rape!

MATT: Ah. What swordplay!

(*As he pantomimes slashing.*)

Ah ha! — Now, that was really living!

LUISA: That handsome bandit — ah, what hands! He grabbed me — here! I've put a little ribbon on the spot.

(*She holds it up for audience to see.*)

MATT: Hot-blooded bandits!
And I cut them down like wheat!
Ha! Ah! Hah!

HUCK: I could speak, but I won't.

BELL: It's tempting, but we shouldn't.

LUISA: It should be made into an epic poem.

MATT: I'll write it.

LUISA: Or better yet — a shrine.

MATT: Divine! I'll build it.

LUISA: Where the wall was.

MATT: This very spot I heard your call,
And here beside our fathers' wall,
I drew my sword and slew them all.
How many — twenty?

LUISA: Thirty!

MATT: Yes! — Or even thirty-two.
And every one there was to slay,
I slew!

(And LUISA swoons in his arms. As they stand there in this romantic pose, HUCKLEBEE speaks with suppressed fury.)

HUCK: Ass.

MATT: I beg your pardon?

HUCK: I say that you're an ass!

MATT: *(Laughs.)*
Charming!

LUISA: *(Also laughing.)*
Isn't it? He behaves like a pantaloon!

(And this sends them both into gales of laughter.)

HUCK: By God, that does it!

BELL: Wait!

HUCK: No. I'm no pantaloon!

(To the children.)

You think that walls come tumbling down?
You think that brigands find an open gate —
The way prepared — You think it's Fate?

MATT: What do you mean?

HUCK: You think that fathers play the fool
To children barely out of school?

LUISA: They do in books.

HUCK: In books, maybe.
It's not the same in reality.
No, children —
Children act on puppet stages
Prepared by parents' hard-won wages.
Or do you think such things can be?
You think a First Class Rape comes free!
By God, look at that, it's the villain's fee!

MATT: What is this?

BELL: An itemized bill for your pretty little Rape.

LUISA: But the feud?

HUCK: We arranged it.

MATT: And the wall?

BELL: Built to fall.

MATT: I don't believe it.

HUCK: Read on, Macduff!

MATT: (*Reads.*)
"Item — a silver piece for actor to portray Indian Raiding Party — body paint included." "Item — a piece of gold to the famous El Gallo."

(*He pronounces is Gal-oh, like the wine.*)

HUCK: (*Taking some pleasure in correcting him.*)
Gay-oh.

MATT: — Gay-oh. — "For allowing himself to seem wounded by a beardless, callow boy."

(*He looks at LUISA, a bit discontented.*)

"Item — one moon —"

(*Looks at the FATHERS.*)

I see you spared no pains.

LUISA: You mean it wasn't real? The bandit? The moon-light — ?

MATT: Everything!

LUISA: But it isn't fair. We didn't need your moon, or bandits. We're in love! We could have made our own moons!

BELL: (*Touched.*)
My child.

MATT: (*Turns to her as it sinks in.*)
We were just puppets!

LUISA: A marriage of convenience!

(*They look at each other, horrified, and then turn their backs and walk to opposite sides of the stage.*)

BELL: (*To HUCKLEBEE.*)
You see. You've spoiled everything!

HUCK: I told you it wouldn't work.

BELL: You told? You? Why, you liar. Get out of my kumquat!

(*And he gives HUCKLEBEE a shove.*)

HUCK: Damn your kumquat!

(*He clips it down to the ground and BELLOMY gasps.*)

BELL: That does it! You're a murderer!

HUCK: And you're a fool!

BELL: (*Rushing over to HUCKLEBEE's garden and turning his watering can upside down.*)
Drown! Drown!

HUCK: (*Rushing to him and giving him a shove.*)
Stop that! You aquamaniac!

BELL: You — you cliptomaniac!

(*They struggle briefly. EL GALLO jumps up on the platform, looking at the FATHERS.*)

By God, that does it! I'm going to build up my wall!

HUCK: I, too!

BELL: I'll lime up mine with bottles!

HUCK: I'll jag mine up with glass!

(*The FATHERS hold up their watering can and clippers as if they were swords, and as they prepare to battle, EL GALLO speaks forcefully.*)

EL GALLO: Pardon me.

FATHERS: Damn!

(*And they exit. EL GALLO starts to leave, but MATT calls out and EL GALLO stops.*)

MATT: Wait!

LUISA: Oh, look! It's my bandit.

MATT: You are —

(*Looks at the bill.*)

El Gayo?

EL GALLO: (*Flipping the red scarf outside his shirt collar.*)
Sometimes.

MATT: About this bill. I think you earned it rather easily.

EL GALLO: You made it rather easy to earn.

MATT: That's true. But now I will make it harder. Where is my sword? Somebody get me a sword!

EL GALLO: Nice boy.

(The MUTE suddenly appears with a real sword and puts it in MATT's hand. MATT looks at it in surprise, then swings it around to hear the slashing sound.)

MATT: En garde!

(Strikes the fencer's basic pose.)

EL GALLO: *(As MATT follows his instructions and he casually defends himself with his naked hand, like a master giving a lesson in swordplay.)*
           Up a bit with the wrist.
           That foot back more.
           Aim at the entrails.
           That's good: encore!
           Thrust One — Thrust Two;
           Bend the knee — Thrust Three!
           But then be sure to parry —
           Like this, see.

(EL GALLO disarms MATT and hands the sword back to the MUTE.)

           Another lesson?

(MATT merely hangs his head in shame, so EL GALLO goes on off, pausing first to tip his hat to LUISA before he leaves.)

MATT: God, I'm a fool!

LUISA: Always bragging.

MATT: Don't be sarcastic.

LUISA: I shall be sarcastic whenever I choose.

MATT: You think I couldn't do it?

LUISA: *(Admiring the ribbon on her wrist.)*
           I think you'd better grow up.

MATT: Grow up! Grow up!

(*To the audience.*)

And this from a girl who is sixteen!

LUISA: Girls mature faster.

MATT: No. This can't be happening.
If I'm not mad,
If I'm not gloriously insane,
Then I'm just me again.
And if I'm me —
Then I can see.

LUISA: What?

MATT: Everything. All the flaws.
You're childish.

LUISA: Child-like.

MATT: Silly.

LUISA: Soulful.

MATT: And you have freckles!

LUISA: (*Suddenly outraged.*)
That's a lie!

MATT: I can see them under those pounds of powder.
Look. Freckles!

LUISA: I hate you!

MATT: You see: self deception. It's a sign of immaturity to
wear lavender perfume before you're forty.

LUISA: You're a poseur. I've heard you talking in the garden, walking around reciting romantic poems about
yourself. Ha — the bold hero!

MATT: You're adolescent!

LUISA: Ahh!

(*She slaps him. There is a pause. Then as they speak,
their anger is underscored by MUSIC.*)

MATT: Beyond that road lies adventure!

LUISA: I'm going to take my hair down and go swimming
in a stream.

MATT: You'll never hear of me again, my dear. I've decided to be bad.

(*EL GALLO appears in the shadows behind them.*)

LUISA: I'll sit up all night and sing songs to the moon!

MATT: I'll drink and gamble! I'll grow a moustache! I'll find my madness — somewhere; out there!

LUISA: I'll find mine, too. I'll have an affair!

MATT: Good-bye forever!

LUISA: See if I care!

(*They break and start to run off, but they suddenly stop — frozen in their tracks — as EL GALLO leaps onto the platform and snaps his fingers. He looks at them understandingly, then he goes to LUISA and picks a tear from her cheek. The Lights, by the way, have gone to black, except for two pools of light on the BOY and GIRL.*)

EL GALLO: This tear is enough — this tiny tear —

(*He carefully puts it in his pocket.*)

A boy may go;
The girl must stay.
Thus runs the world away.

(*LUISA crosses to the platform and sits, facing upstage. MATT is still frozen, caught in the middle of a dream. EL GALLO steps up on the platform and looks at him.*)

See, he sees it.
And the world seems very grand.

(*The MUSIC has begun and now MATT sings as EL GALLO echoes him cynically.*)

MATT: Beyond that road lies a shining world.

EL GALLO: Beyond that road lies despair.

MATT: Beyond that road lies a world that's gleaming.

EL GALLO: People who are scheming.

MATT: Beauty!

EL GALLO: Hunger!

MATT: Glory!

EL GALLO: Sorrow!

MATT: Never a pain or care.

EL GALLO: He's liable to find a couple of surprises there.

      There's a song he must sing;
      It's a well-known song.
      But the tune is bitter
      And it doesn't take long to learn!

MATT: I can learn!

EL GALLO: That pretty little world that beams so bright.
      That pretty little world that seems delightful
      Can burn! — burn! — burn!

MATT: Let me learn! Let me learn!

      For, I can see it!
      Shining somewhere!
      Bright lights somewhere invite me to come there
      And learn!
      And I'm ready!

      I can hear it!
      Sirens singing!
      Inside my ear I hear them all singing
      Come learn!

      Who knows — maybe —
      All the visions that I see
      May be waiting just for me
      To say — take me there, and

      Make me see it!
      Make me feel it!
      I know it's so
      I know that it really
      May be!
      Let me learn!

      I can see it!

EL GALLO: He can see it!

MATT: Shining somewhere!

EL GALLO: Shining somewhere!

Those lights not only glitter but once there they
    burn!

MATT: I can hear it!

EL GALLO: He can hear it.

MATT: Sirens singing!

EL GALLO: Sirens singing.

Don't listen close or maybe you'll never
Return!

BOTH: Who knows — may be
All the visions I (he) can see
May be waiting just for me (him) to—

EL GALLO: *(He raises his hands as if casting a spell on the BOY.)*
Say —

MATT: I can see it!

EL GALLO: Say —

MATT: Shining somewhere!

EL GALLO: Say —

MATT: Let me see it!

EL GALLO: Say —

MATT: Take me there
And make me a part of it!

Make me see
Those shining sights inside of me!

EL GALLO: Make him see it!

MATT: Make me feel
Those lights inside
Don't lie to me!

EL GALLO: Make him feel it!

BOTH: I (he) know(s) it's so —
I (he) know(s) that it really may be!

MATT: Just what I've always waited for!
This is what my life's created for!

BOTH: Let me (him) learn!

EL GALLO: *(Speaks when the MUSIC is over.)*
The world will teach him
Very quickly
The secret he needs to know.
A certain parable about Romance;
And so —
We let him go.
We commit him to the tender mercies
Of that most stringent teacher — Time.
But . . .
Just so there's no slip-up
We'll add a bit — of spice.

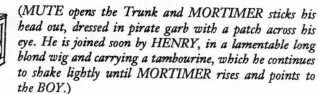

(MUTE opens the Trunk and MORTIMER sticks his head out, dressed in pirate garb with a patch across his eye. He is joined soon by HENRY, in a lamentable long blond wig and carrying a tambourine, which he continues to shake lightly until MORTIMER rises and points to the BOY.)

MORT: Hold on there a minute, Matie!

MATT: What?

HENRY: And where may you be going, my fiery-eyed young friend? Don't bother to answer; I can see it in your eyes!

MORT: I see it, too — them beady little eyes!

HENRY: You go for the goose — the golden goose that lays the platinum-plated egg, right?

MORT: Right!

HENRY: I am Lodevigo. Just like yourself — a young man looking for the pleasant pinch of adventure.

(He adjusts his ratty wig. HENRY, by the way, has painted his lips bright crimson for this scene. And darkened his eyebrows. And thickened his lashes. And painted on a beauty spot.)

MATT: Young man?

HENRY: Yes!

(Strikes a pose, showing off his scrawny leg.)

And to your left, observe this seamy individual. He

is my companion who goes by the name of — Socrates.

MORT: (*Steps close to MATT and breathes on him.*)
I'm Roman.

HENRY: Romanoff, he means. A blue-blood.
He is descended from the T-zars.

MATT: The T-zars?

HENRY: Yes. The T-zars! He is, in fact, the noblest Romanoff of them all. But enough of this chit-chat.

MORT: Enough. Enough.

HENRY: You long for adventure? We will take you, won't we, Socci?

MORT: We'll take him, all right!

HENRY: To the places you've dreamed of — Venice — Egypt! Ah Egypt! "I am dying; Egypt!"

(*HENRY falls to the floor dramatically. Then he rises and speaks to the audience.*)

That's a line from something, I don't recall just what.

MATT: I thought I would —

HENRY: Seek your fortune! Exactly why we're here. Right, Socci?

MORT: Right, Loddi. We're going to give you the works!

HENRY: The fireworks, he means.

MATT: It was my intention —

HENRY: Forget intentions! They paved the road to hell! We'll see to your education.

MORT: We know all the ropes!

HENRY: And the ropes to skip as well!

MORT: 'Eathen idols!

HENRY: Whirling girlies!

MORT: Tipsy Gypsies!

HENRY: Fantastic beauty!
Just waiting to be —

(*MORTIMER makes a zipper sound.*)

Unzipped!

MATT: But I —

HENRY: (*As he and MORTIMER both clap hands over MATT's mouth.*)
Don't bother to thank us!

(*Calls out to the PIANIST.*)

Maestro!

(*And they sing as they up-end the BOY and carry him out.*)

HENRY &
  MORT: Beyond that road's an episode —
An episode —
An episode.
Beyond that road lies an episode

HENRY: Look out; you nearly tripped!

MORT: Hip! Hip!

BOTH: Beyond that road's an episode —
An episode —
An episode.
Beyond that road lies an episode
Just waiting to be unzipped!

(*As they exit, they sing lustily, mocking MATT and EL GALLO's earlier song.*)

I can see it!
Shining somewhere!

(*When they have gone, EL GALLO takes down the Sun and stands with the Moon side facing the audience. The MUTE gets the grey cloth and, as EL GALLO speaks, the MUTE crosses the stage carrying the long grey cloth of china silk.*)

EL GALLO: Now grant me in your minds a month.
October is over and the sky grows grey.
A month goes by,

It's a little bit colder.
A month goes by.
We're one month older.

(Enter BELLOMY wearing his winter scarf.)

BELL: *(To the MUTE, who is kneeling by the Bench.)*
That's fine. There's nothing better than a good thick wall. Keep working, friend. Keep working.

(He exits and HUCKLEBEE comes in. He, too, sports his winter garb.)

HUCK: *(Coming over to MUTE.)*
Still progressing? Good. We want to get it finished before snowfall.

(He exits and BELLOMY returns.)

BELL: Hmmm. Getting colder. I'll just take a look at the wall.

(Crosses over to MUTE.)

Fine! Keep on working.

(To audience.)

Lord, this weather makes a man feel old.

(Exits.)

HUCK: *(Re-entering.)*
Not a word. He's been gone for a month, and I haven't had a single word.

(To the MUTE.)

How's it going? Hmmm?

(MUTE gives him a look.)

Oh. I forgot. You're not supposed to talk.

BELL: *(Entering and crossing to LUISA, carrying blue scarf in both hands.)*
Luisa? — Now, dear, listen. It's silly to stand in the garden. You'll catch pneumonia. You'll catch asthma. Luisa?

(No response.)

Well, anyway — I brought you a little shawl.

(BELLOMY drapes the shawl over LUISA's head, then he moves to the Bench. The FATHERS see each other. They hesitate, and then bow gravely. Then BELLOMY speaks to the MUTE.)

BELL: I don't suppose you'd care to see my garden?

HUCK: He won't answer.

BELL: I don't recall addressing that remark to you, sir.

HUCK: He's not supposed to speak.

BELL: Oh — Oh, well.

(EL GALLO nods to the MUTE, then exits. The MUTE grabs the grey cloth, steps on to the platform, turns front, and "snaps" the grey cloth. Then he follows EL GALLO off to the side. Both FATHERS grab their shoulders and shiver at the snap of the cloth. Then BELLOMY speaks.)

BELL: By the way.

HUCK: Yes?

BELL: Oh — nothing.

(HUCKLBEE begins to chuckle.)

BELL: What's so funny?

HUCK: I was just thinking how we used to meet.

BELL: Climbing over the wall.

HUCK: Secret meetings —

BELL: Just to play a little game of cards.

(They both laugh. Then BELLOMY speaks seriously.)

How's your son?

HUCK: Not a word.

BELL: He'll be back — when he runs out of your money.

HUCK: Thank you. And your daughter?

BELL: Like a statue. Does nothing but dream all day.

HUCK: Pity. — How's your garden?

BELL: Growing!

HUCK: Mine, too.

BELL: So dependable.
Gardens go on growing.

HUCK: Yes, indeed, they do.

BELL: I tell you, I love vegetables.

HUCK: It's true. I love them, too.

(*They shake hands and sing.*)

BELL: Plant a radish.
Get a radish.
Never any doubt.
That's why I love vegetables;
You know what you're about!

HUCK: Plant a turnip.
Get a turnip.
Maybe you'll get two.
That's why I love vegetables;
You know that they'll come through!

BELL: They're dependable!

HUCK: They're befriendable!

BOTH: They're the best pal a parent's ever known!

BELL: While with children,

HUCK: It's bewilderin'.

BOTH: You don't know until the seed is nearly grown

BELL: Just what you've sown.

BOTH: So
Plant a carrot,
Get a carrot,

HUCK: Not a brussel sprout.

BOTH: That's why I love vegetables.
You know what you're about!

BELL: Life is merry,

HUCK: If it's very

BOTH: Vegetarian!

A man who plants a garden
Is a very happy man!

(This second chorus they sing like a vaudeville team complete with little dance steps.)

HUCK: Plant a beanstalk.
Get a beanstalk.
Just the same as Jack.
Then if you don't like it,
You can always take it back!

BELL: But if your issue
Doesn't kiss you,
Then I wish you luck.
For once you've planted children,
You're absolutely stuck!

BOTH: Every turnip green!
Every kidney bean!
Every plant grows according to the plot!

HUCK: While with progeny,

BELL: It's hodge-podgenee.

BOTH: For as soon as you think you know what kind you've got,

BELL: It's what they're not!

BOTH: So —
Plant a cabbage.
Get a cabbage.

HUCK: Not a sauerkraut!

BOTH: That's why I love vegetables.
You know what you're about!

Life is merry
If it's very
Vegetarian.

A man who plants a garden
Is a very happy man!

HUCK: A vegetari —

BELL: Very merry —

BOTH: Vegetarian!

(*When song is over, during the applause, they turn to each other and shake hands.*)

BELL: Say, what about that little game of cards? Pinochle?

HUCK: I prefer poker.

BELL: All right, but let's hurry!

HUCK: You still owe me from last time.

(*To the MUTE.*)

You keep on working.

BELL: He's a nice chap.

HUCK: (*Looking down at the MUTE noncommittally.*)
Umm.

(*And they exit. LUISA, meanwhile, has begun to come out of her trance.*)

LUISA : (*Sings as Light comes up on her.*)
I'd like to swim in a clear blue stream
Where the water is icy cold.
Then go to town in a golden gown
And have my fortune told.

EL GALLO: (*Sings as Light comes up on him*)
Just once.
Just once.
Just once before you're old . . .

LUISA: It's my bandit!

EL GALLO: Your bandit, yes.

LUISA: What are you doing up in that tree?

EL GALLO: Growing ripe.

LUISA: Don't grow too ripe or you'll fall.

EL GALLO: Very wise.

LUISA: What do you see from up there?

EL GALLO: Everything.

LUISA: Really?

EL GALLO: Nearly.

LUISA: Do you see Matt?

EL GALLO: Do you care?

LUISA: No. I just wondered.
Can I climb up there beside you?

EL GALLO: You can if you can.

LUISA: (*Climbs up beside him. The stage is dark now, and only the "tree" is lit.*)
There! I don't see everything.

EL GALLO: It takes a little while.

LUISA: All I see is my own house. And Matt's. And the wall.

EL GALLO: And that's all?

LUISA: All. Is it fun to be a bandit?

EL GALLO: It has its moments.

LUISA: I think it must be fun. Tell me, do you ride on a great white horse?

EL GALLO: I used to.

LUISA: But no longer?

EL GALLO: I developed a saddle rash. Very painful.

LUISA: How unglamorous. I never heard of a hero who had a saddle rash.

EL GALLO: Oh, it happens. Occupational hazard.

LUISA: Tell me: What is your favorite plunder?

EL GALLO: Plunder? I think that's Pirates.

LUISA: Well then, booty.

EL GALLO: You've been reading too many books.

LUISA: Well, you must steal something!

EL GALLO: Oh, yes. I steal fancies. I steal whatever is treasured most.

LUISA: That's more like it.
Precious rubies!

EL GALLO: (*Looking at her necklace.*)
Precious rhinestones.

LUISA: Rhinestones?

EL GALLO: Can be precious.
It depends on the point of view.

LUISA: Well, it doesn't sound very sound.
Economically, I mean.

EL GALLO: (*Touched, in spite of himself.*)
Pretty child.

LUISA: Do you think so? Do I attract you?

EL GALLO: Somewhat.

LUISA: Oh. But that's splendid!
Look, see this ribbon?
That's where you gave me a bruise.

EL GALLO: I'm so sorry.

LUISA: Don't be silly. I adore it!
I kiss it three times every day.
Tell me. Have you seen the world?

EL GALLO: A bit, yes.

LUISA: Is it like in the books?

EL GALLO: It depends on which books you read.

LUISA: The Adventures. The Romances.
"Cast off thy name. A rose by any other name —"
Do you know that?

EL GALLO: Sounds familiar.

LUISA: "Put up thy sword. The dew will rust it!"
That's Othello. He was older than Desdemona,
But she loved him because he had seen the world.
Of course, he killed her.

EL GALLO: Of course.

LUISA: (*Deeply touched.*)
"It is a far better thing that I do now than I have
ever done before!" Isn't that beautiful? That man
was beheaded.

EL GALLO:	(*Not deeply touched.*) I'm not surprised.
LUISA:	Take me there!
EL GALLO:	Where?
LUISA:	To the parties! To the world!
EL GALLO:	But I'm a bandit. There is a price upon my head.
LUISA:	Oh! I was hoping there would be!

(*MUSIC.*)

| EL GALLO: | You and I!
Us together! |
| LUISA: | Yes.Dancing forever and forever! |

(*As EL GALLO sings, he holds his hand above her, her eyes closed — as if casting her in a trance.*)

EL GALLO:
Round and round,
Till the break of day.
Candles glow,
Fiddles play.
Why not be wild if we feel that way?
Reckless and terribly gay!

Round and round,
'Neath a magic spell.
Velvet gown,
Pink lapel.
Life is a colorful carousel.

Reckless and terribly gay!

(*EL GALLO raises his hand. She lifts her head and her eyes suddenly open.*)

LUISA:
I'm ready anytime.
If you'll take me, I'm
Ready to go!

So show the way to me.
I will try to be
Ready to go!

EL GALLO: I seem to see Venice:

We're on a lagoon.
A gondolier's crooning
A gondola tune.
The air makes your hair
Billow blue in the moon!

LUISA: I could swoon!

EL GALLO: You're so blue in the moon!

(And now they begin to dance. The MUTE hands her a mask — a plastic mask of a laughing-hollow face that is frozen forever into unutterable joy. This mask is upon a little hand-stick, so that when held in front of one's visage, it blocks out any little tell-tale traces of compassion or of horror.)

(As LUISA and EL GALLO go on dancing, we see — in a stylized blaze of light — MORTIMER and HENRY up on the platform, now transformed into a puppet-like stage, waving "flames" of torn red silk. At first they are gondoliers, but as the action gets wilder, they change into rioting peasants. In each of these sequences, it is MATT who is the object of their fury.)

(At EL GALLO's urging, LUISA takes the mask and holds it up to her face.)

LUISA: *(Speaks as she looks through mask.)*
Look at the peasants!
They're lighting candelabras.
No. I believe they're lighting torches.
Yes, see —
They've started burning the palaces!

There goes the Doge!

HENRY: Arrivederci!

LUISA: What fun! I adore pyrotechnics!

(MATT slowly rises, writhing, as HENRY and MORTIMER turn to him, and billow their "flames" up and down his twisting body. LUISA puts down her mask and speaks to EL GALLO.)

LUISA: That man — look out; he's burning. My God, he's on fire!

EL GALLO: (*Pleasantly.*)
Keep on dancing.

LUISA: But he's burning!

EL GALLO: Just put up your mask.
Then it's pretty.

(*LUISA puts on mask.*)

MATT: Help!

LUISA: Oh. Yes, isn't he beautiful!
He's all sort of orange.
Red-orange.
That's one of my favorite colors.

MATT: (*Writhing in pain.*)
Help!

LUISA: You look lovely!

(*With one last flash of flame, HENRY and MORTI-MER pull MATT down out of sight on the little "puppet stage."*)

EL GALLO: (*As LUISA sings a wild obbligato.*)
We'll just dance!
We'll kick up our heels to music and dance!
Until my head reels with music.
Just like a lovely real romance.
All we'll do is daily dance.

All we'll do is just dance.
All we'll do is just dance.
All we'll do is just —

LUISA: (*Speaks.*)
Whee. I'm exhausted.

EL GALLO: But you can't be.
The evening's just started!

(*MUSIC. As he sings, LUISA turns slowly round and round on the Prop Box, the mask up to her face, like a mechanical doll.*)

Round and round
Till the break of day.
Candles glow.

Fiddles play.
Why not be wild if we feel that way?
Reckless and terribly gay!

LUISA: I'm ready anytime,
If you'll take me, I'm
Ready to go!

So show the way to me;
I will try to be
Ready to go!

EL GALLO: I seem to see Athens, it's terribly chic.
Atop the Acrop'lis, it's terribly Greek.
There's Venus, Adonis, 'n us — cheek to cheek.

(*As Venus and Adonis have been mentioned, HENRY and MORTIMER pop out from behind the "puppet stage," trying to look Greek.*)

LUISA: Oh how chic!

EL GALLO: To be Greek cheek to cheek!

(*Once again MATT rises into sight.*)

LUISA: Observe the friendly natives!

HENRY &
MORT: (*Waving their "whips" of colored ribbons at the audience.*)
Hello there!

LUISA: La, how gay.

(*HENRY and MORTIMER turn up to MATT and begin to "whip" him in rhythm with their streamers.*)

Look, dear, they're beating a monkey.
Isn't it fun.

(*Puts down mask; looks at EL GALLO.*)

I wonder why anyone should be beating a monkey?

(*Looks front.*)

Oh, no, that's it.
It's not a monkey at all.
It's a man dressed in a monkey suit.
That man — they've hurt him!

EL GALLO: Put up the mask.

LUISA: But he is wounded!

EL GALLO: The mask! The mask!

(Once again she lifts the mask up to her face.)

MATT: Help!

LUISA: Oh, isn't that cute.
They're beating a man in a monkey suit.
It's a show. La, how jolly.
Don't stop; it's charming.
Don't stop.

MATT: Help!

LUISA: That's it. Writhe some more!

(The "puppets" disappear again, as EL GALLO and LUISA dance.)

EL GALLO: *(Sings as LUISA resumes her obbligato.)*
We'll just dance!
We'll kick up our heels to music and dance!
Until my head reels with music.
Just like a lovely real romance.
All we'll do is daily dance.

All we'll do is just dance.
All we'll do is just dance.
All we'll do is just —

LUISA: Couldn't we just sit this one out?

EL GALLO: Ridiculous! When there's music to be danced to.
Play, Gypsies!

(Shouts are heard from behind the "puppet stage." Then everyone, including the OLD ACTORS, joins in singing.)

EL GALLO
(& ALL):   Round and round
'Neath the magic spell.
Velvet gown.
Pink lapel.
Life is a colorful carousel.
Reckless and terribly gay.

| LUISA: | I'm ready anytime,
If you'll take me, I'm
Ready to go!

So show the way to me;
I will try to be
Ready to go | EL G.: | Gay —
We're so gay!
Terribly gay!

Gay —
We're so gay!
Terribly gay! |

EL GALLO: We'll be in Bengasi or maybe Bombay.
I understand Indja is terribly gay.
The natives assemble on feast day and play

LUISA: With their snakes!

EL GALLO: What a racket it makes!

LUISA: I think I'm going to love Indja.
Such a big population, and
I adore crowds!
Oh, look, there's a fakir —
Hi, fakir!

HENRY: (*A bit confused.*)
Arrivederci!

LUISA: See — he's there with his assistants.
They all know Yogi —
And they're just loads of fun!
There's one — a young one —
There're putting him down on some nails.

(*She puts down her mask.*)

If he fails,
He'll be cut to bits by those nails.

MATT: Help!

LUISA: Someone help him.

EL GALLO: The mask!

LUISA: But he's bleeding!
Horrible!

EL GALLO: Mask!

(*And he forces it up to her face. Once more, the transition.*)

LUISA: Go on. Sit down harder!
He's a sissy.

I don't believe he's a real fakir.
They never complain.
He's a fake fakir.

MATT: Help!

LUISA: Fake!

(And we go into the last chorus, with LUISA singing the obbligato and the entire company — except the MUTE — singing in the background.)

EL GALLO: *(As the others sing their variations.)*
We'll —
Just —
Dance—!

We'll kick up our heels to music
And dance!
Until my head reels with music.
Just like a lovely real romance —

(HENRY and MORTIMER come forward and kneel on either side of LUISA, joined by the MUTE who comes with his red flame and kneels just below her. As they do so, all three continue to move their flames up and down, so they are licking LUISA's body as she turns round and round, the laughing mask barely covering her own horrified face.)

All we'll do is daily —
I can see the friendly natives!
All we'll do is just dance!
All we'll do is just dance!
All we'll do is just —
Round and round in a magic spell —

(The OLD ACTORS and the MUTE rush back up to the platform and resume flaming the BOY as LUISA stops turning and stands facing front, her face just below EL GALLO's.)

All we'll do is just —
All we'll do is just —
All we'll do is just —
All we'll do is just —

EL GALLO
  & LUISA: All we'll do is just

MATT: *(Calls out.)*
HELP!

EL GALLO
& ALL: Dance!

(At the end of the number, HENRY, MORTIMER and MATT have all gone, and LUISA and EL GALLO are back in the "tree," exactly like the scene before.)

(When the Lights come back up, the feeling is dark and somber. The MUSIC softly picks up a delicate, eerie underscoring of "Round and Round.")

EL GALLO: *(Taking the mask from her.)*
Now hurry. You must pack so that we may run away.

LUISA: Kiss me first.

EL GALLO: All right.

LUISA: Ahh.

EL GALLO: What is it?

LUISA: At last! I have been kissed upon the eyes. No matter what happens, I'll never forget that kiss. I'll go now.

EL GALLO: One word, Luisa, listen:
I want to tell you this —
I promise to remember, too
That one particular kiss.

And now hurry; we have a lifetime for kisses!

LUISA: True. You'll wait here?

EL GALLO: I promise.

LUISA: All right, then.

EL GALLO: Wait! Give me a trinket — to pledge that you will come back. That necklace —

LUISA: Was my mother's.

EL GALLO: Good. It will serve as your pledge.

(He holds out his hand. She considers, then removes necklace and places it gently in his hand.)

LUISA: All right. I leave you this necklace because it is my favorite thing. Here, guard it. I won't be long.

(*She starts to go and then turns back.*)

It's really like that? The world is like you say?

EL GALLO: Of course.

(*EL GALLO moves to pole, alongside LUISA, and points "off." As he sings, and the BOY echoes, LUISA remains transfixed, gazing at the distant point.*)

EL GALLO: Beyond that road lies a shining world.

MATT: (*Appearing, dirty and disheveled.*)
Beyond that road lies despair.

EL GALLO: Beyond that road lies a world that's gleaming.

MATT: People who are scheming.

EL GALLO: Beauty!

MATT: Hunger!

EL GALLO: Glory!

MATT: Sorrow!

EL GALLO: Never a pain or care.

MATT: She's liable to find a couple of surprises there.

LUISA: I'm ready. I won't be long.

(*Once more, she turns back.*)

You will be here?

EL GALLO: Right here. I promise.

(*When LUISA has gone, EL GALLO wraps his hand around the necklace. Then he turns to exit quickly, but he is interrupted by MATT.*)

MATT: Wait!

EL GALLO: Well. The Prodigal Son comes home.

MATT: Don't leave her like that.
It isn't fair.

EL GALLO: It's her misfortune.
What do you care?

MATT: She's too young.
I said, don't leave her!

(MATT tries to stop him. EL GALLO raises his hand sharply and, as if struck, the BOY falls back against the pole, and then slowly sinks into a sitting position on the platform, his head bowed. Then EL GALLO moves on off into the shadows, out of sight.)

(LUISA returns. She calls out for EL GALLO, but he isn't there. Suddenly, as if by some quick instinct, she realizes she has been left. Slowly, sadly, she sits on the platform and bows her head.)

(EL GALLO returns and moves to the center of the platform to address the audience.)

EL GALLO: There is a curious paradox
That no one can explain.
Who understands the secret
Of the reaping of the grain?

Who understands why Spring is born
Out of Winter's laboring pain?
Or why we all must die a bit
Before we grow again.

I do not know the answer.
I merely know it's true.
I hurt them for that reason;
And myself a little bit, too.

(He steps back into the shadows.)

MATT: It isn't worth tears, believe me.
Luisa, please — don't cry.

LUISA: You look awful.

MATT: I know.

LUISA: What's that swelling?

MATT: That's my eye.

LUISA: And those scratches.
What in the world happened to you?

MATT: The world happened to me.

LUISA: Did you drink and gamble?

MATT: The first day, yes.
But the drink was drugged,

And the wheel kept hitting sixes.
Until I played a six.

LUISA: Did you serenade señoras?

MATT: I did for a little while.
Until I got hit.

LUISA: Hit?

MATT: With a slop pot.

LUISA: What?

MATT: A Spanish slop pot.
Believe me, it defies description.

(*She cannot help but smile at this.*)

LUISA: I'm sorry, Matt.

MATT: No. It's all right. I deserve it.
I've been foolish.

LUISA: I have, too. Believe me.
More than you.

(*Simply — very simply — they sit facing forward and sing.*)

MATT: When the moon was young,
When the month was May,
When the stage was hung for my holiday,
I saw shining lights
But I never knew:
They were you.
They were you.
They were you.

LUISA: When the dance was done,
When I went my way,
When I tried to find rainbows far away,
All the lovely lights seemed to fade from view:
They were you.
They were you.
They were you.

BOTH: Without you near me,
I can't see.
When you're near me,
Wonderful things come to be.

MATT: Every secret prayer,

LUISA: Every fancy free,

MATT: Everything I dared for both

BOTH: You and me.

          All my wildest dreams
          Multiplied by two —

MATT: They were you.

LUISA: They were you.

BOTH: They were you.

LUISA: They were you.

MATT: They were you.

BOTH: They were you.

LUISA: *(Speaks as the MUSIC continues.)*
          I missed you, Matt.

MATT: I missed you, too.

LUISA: Oh. You've been hurt.

MATT: Yes.

LUISA: But you should have told me.
          You should have told me right away.
          Here, sit down.
          Maybe I can bind it.

          (MATT sits as LUISA kneels beside him and the MUTE appears above them.)

MATT: *(Taking her face in his hands, and looking at her intently.)*
          You've been hurt, too.

LUISA: Yes.

          (The MUTE begins to sprinkle them with white confetti.)

MATT: Look. It's beginning to snow.

LUISA: I know.

MATT: Here. Take my coat.

LUISA: No. Both.
          There's room enough for both.

(They pull close together as the MUTE continues to sprinkle "snow," and they sing.)

BOTH: Love.
You are love.
   (You are love.)
Better far than a metaphor
Can ever, ever be.

Love.
   (You are love.)
You are love
   (You are love.)
My mystery —
   (My mystery —)
Of love!

(And the FATHERS, who have been sitting upstage, now rise and come forward.)

BELL: Look!

EL GALLO: Shh.

HUCK: They've come back!

BELL: It's a miracle. Let's take down the wall.

EL GALLO: No. Leave the wall.
Remember —
You must always leave the wall.

(Sings, as the others hum.)

Deep in December, it's nice to remember,
Although you know the snow will follow.
Deep in December, it's nice to remember:
Without a hurt the heart is hollow.
Deep in December, it's nice to remember
The fire of September that made us mellow.
Deep in December, our hearts should remember,
And follow.

(The MUTE gets the FANTASTICKS drape from the Prop Box and he and EL GALLO carefully hang it on the poles in front of the PARENTS and the LOVERS. Then, when the stage is as it was in the beginning, the Lights dim down. And the play, of course, is done.)

THE END

3

A Scrapbook

About The Authors

Tom Jones and Harvey Schmidt wrote *The Fantasticks* in 1959 for a summer production at Barnard College in New York. Since its Off-Broadway opening at the Sullivan Street Playhouse in May 1960, it has gone on to become the longest running musical in the world and the longest running show in the history of the American theatre.

Next came a musical version of N. Richard Nash's play *The Rainmaker*, entitled *110 in the Shade*. It was their first Broadway show, and its score was singled out by the critics and nominated for a Tony Award. Their two-character musical *I Do! I Do!*, starring Mary Martin and Robert Preston, was a great success on Broadway and on the road, where it was revived with Carol Burnett and Rock Hudson.

For several years Jones and Schmidt worked privately at Portfolio, their own theatre workshop in New York, concentrating on small-scale musicals in new and often untried forms. The most notable of these efforts were *Celebration*, which moved on to Broadway, and *Philemon*, which won an Outer Critics Circle Award and then was later produced by Hollywood Television Theatre.

Among their new works are *Grover's Corners*, a musical version of Thornton Wilder's Pulitzer Prize-winning play *Our Town*, and an original musical based on the life of the great French writer, Colette. The Thirtieth Anniversary Tour of *The Fantasticks* starring Robert Goulet launched its forty week run across the United States in May, 1990.

TOM JONES (left) and HARVEY SCHMIDT (right) on stage at the Sullivan Street Playhouse

(Photo/Martha Swope)

The
Fantasticks

THE
FANTASTICKS

THE
FANTASTICKS

THE
FANTASTICKS

THE
FANTASTICKS

THE
FANTASTICKS

The
Fantasticks

A selection of possible logos for the show submitted by HARVEY SCHMIDT to producer LORE NOTO in 1960. The bottom one, in Schmidt's handwriting, was the one chosen.

About "The Fantasticks"

As it celebrates its thirtieth anniversary at the Sullivan Street Playhouse in New York, *The Fantasticks* (Book & Lyrics: Tom Jones; Music: Harvey Schmidt) is not only the longest running musical in the world, it is also the most frequently produced.

There have been over 11,000 productions in the United States in over 3,000 cities and towns. It has played all fifty states, plus Puerto Rico, the Virgin Islands, and the District of Columbia. It established record runs in Houston, San Francisco, Los Angeles and Denver. There have been 17 productions in the nation's capital, including one which gave a special performance at the White House.

The Fantasticks has had 693 productions in 68 foreign countries. There have been 23 productions in Sweden, 7 in New Zealand, 5 in Saudi Arabia, 4 in Czechoslovakia, and 3 in Israel. It has played Kabul, Afghanistan (before the Russian takeover) and Teheran, Iran (before the Ayatollah). In 1987 it was performed (in Mandarin) by the famed Peking Opera, and in 1988 an American company under the direction of the authors toured Japan and then alternated with the Japanese company which has been playing for 18 years. This year, under the auspices of the State Department, *The Fantasticks* will be played in Russia for the first time.

The New York production has seen seven U.S. presidents, so far. It has survived many newspaper strikes and several of the newspapers that originally reviewed it. It has lived through a blizzard or two, an actors' strike, two blackouts, transportation strikes that crippled the city, a Presidential assassination, a Presidential resignation, and the 1975 knockout of telephone service for approximately three weeks (all Off-Broadway shows depend almost entirely on telephone reservations).

In 1986, when producer Lore Noto became ill, it was decided that the time had come for it to close. A modest ad was placed in *The New York Times* announcing that *The Fantasticks* would close on the evening of Sunday, June 8th. The results were astonishing. The remaining two months were sold out within a week. Letters began to pour in from all over the world protesting the decision. The casts of the Broadway shows signed petitions. Finally, a trusted friend of Noto's, a business-man named Don Thompson, offered to step in and take over as pro-ducer while Noto recovered. Thus, the closing was rescinded, and the show resumed its record breaking run.

The Greenwich Village 19th-Century brick building at 181 Sullivan Street, the current home of the Sullivan Street Playhouse and *The Fantasticks*, was, many years before that, the birthplace of Mayor FIORELLO LA GUARDIA and later the popular nightclub Jimmy Kelly's. JULES FIELD, pictured above, has been the owner during the 30-year tenancy of *The Fantasticks*, and when that show opened, he signed a "Run-of-the-Play" contract, but as years of constant inflation rolled by, it was deemed by all parties involved to be unfair, and a new contract was eventually drawn up.

"Abductions" (And So Forth)

We like to think that *The Fantasticks* does not date. Based as it is upon an ancient sort of story, and utilizing primitive presentational stage devices from around the world, it seems to move easily from one culture to another, from one decade to the next. It was not "contemporary" when it was written. It was not meant to be. And for that reason it has been able to go through a significant number of social and cultural changes without losing its appeal.

Perhaps the one exception to this seeming timelessness is the use of the word "rape." Beginning with the Women's Liberation Movement and increasing steadily over the years, our consciousness has been raised. The word "rape," which seemed so harmless in 1960, seems less harmless now. Of course, the word was never intended in a literal sense, but rather in the dictionary definition: "To seize and carry off by force." (From the Latin "rapere.") Even so, there is no doubt that some of the humor was obtained by the surprise effect, the "naughtiness," of this short, unexpected word.

As noted in the Foreword to this edition, *The Fantasticks* is based upon an early play by Rostand called *Les Romanesques*. In 1900 a British woman, writing under the pseudonym of George Fleming, did a verse translation, calling it *The Fantasticks*. And in that version, it was her "conceit" to have the bandit, Straforel, discuss the possible types of abductions as "rapes," in the spoofing manner of *The Rape of the Lock*.

Later, when we decided to turn the little Rostand piece into a musical, we used the George Fleming version as our source. When we cast Jerry Orbach as El Gallo and realized the extent of both his singing talent and his comedic skills, we decided to take the "Rape Speech" and turn it into the song "It Depends on What You Pay."

This, then, is the history of our dilemma. What is the solution? Indeed, is there any need for a solution? The producers of the original

Sullivan Street production do not think so. They feel that the show has been playing for thirty years without seriously offending anyone and, further, they feel that the very way the word is used makes it clear that we are not talking about "real" rape. We are not so sure, though it is hard to argue with the ongoing success and the continuing absence of any serious complaints.

After much discussion with the Sullivan Street producers, it was finally decided to leave the song untouched, but to alter the introductory scene, making it as clear as possible that we were referring to "artistic," "literary" rape, as in *The Rape of the Lock*.

However, for the new Thirtieth Anniversary tour to be launched in the Spring of 1990, we have written a new song to replace the old one. It is called "Abductions, (And So Forth)," and it is based upon the music of the "Abduction Ballet." This song, both music and lyric, has been made available through Music Theatre International, so that in the future anyone doing the show will have an alternate choice in case they are offended by the word "rape."

We include it here, along with the little scene which precedes it, in order that you may judge for yourself.

Stockholm, Sweden, Lilla Teatern production. Left to right: STEN MATTSSON as Mortimer, WALTER NORMAN as Matt, BRITTA PETTERSSON as Luisa, AKE LAGERGREN as Henry.

ABDUCTIONS

BELL: How much for such a drama?

EL GALLO: That, Señor, depends.

BELL: On what?

EL GALLO: What else? The quality of the "rape."

BELL: Nope.

(*He starts to leave, but EL GALLO intercepts him.*)

EL GALLO: Forgive me. The attempted "rape." The abduction. The seizure. The kidnapping. Call it what you will. To plunder. To pillage. To carry off by force. From the Latin "rapere," meaning "to seize."

BELL: Well, it doesn't sound right to me.

EL GALLO: It is though, I assure you.
As a matter of fact, it's standard.
The lovers meet in secret. And so forth.
A group of villains interrupts them. And so forth.
There is a fight. A reconciliation. A happy ending.
And so forth.
All of it quite standard.

BELL: What about the cost — and so forth?

EL GALLO: Cost goes by type. In your case, I think I would recommend a "First Class."

BELL: You mean, we get a choice?

EL GALLO: Yes, of course. And with regular union rates.

(*Sings.*)

Abductions!
Abductions!
Theatrical abductions!
Complete with maidens in distress
And fabulous productions:
With moonlight — and so forth.
With China silk — and so forth.
The sort of thing you see upon the operatic stage.

Two lovers
Are meeting.

Their happiness is fleeting.
For all at once a band of men
Is standing there, repeating:
"Surrender!" — and so forth.
"Give us the girl!" — and so forth.
In short, they are surrounded by a gang of angry
    men.

HUCK: I see it!
I see it!
A gang of angry men!

EL GALLO: Heaven!
I can assure you, this is heaven!
For six young lovers out of seven,
This is a dream of ecstasy!

Passion!
I'm selling poetry and passion!
And since romance is still the fashion,
It can be furnished for a fee.

HUCK: Can we deny them
Such a dream of ecstasy?

BELL: Sounds a bit expensive.
I would like to know the fee.

EL GALLO: Their leader,
Appearing,
Is standing center, leering.
He wears a cape and sneers a sneer
That's really quite endearing.
He's dashing — and so forth.
A handsome rogue — and so forth.
He steals the girl and starts to carry her into the
    night!

The hero,
He sees her.
He grabs the girl and frees her.
He tweaks the villain by the nose,
Which certainly should please her.
They argue — and so forth.
They draw their swords — and so forth.
They shout "En garde!" — and fight until the bandit
Says, "I die!"

HUCK: They're fighting:
Exciting!
The bandit says, "I die!"

EL GALLO: Drama!
That's what I'm offering; it's drama!
Into life's faded cyclorama,
I try to shed a little light!

Thrilling!
You must admit that this is thrilling.
And it can happen if you're willing
To just make sure the price is right.

HUCK: It's so exciting!
He could shed a little light!

BELL: Yes, it's quite exciting,
But what sort of price is right?

EL GALLO: The parents,
Relenting,
Rush on the scene, presenting
A perfect picture of content
With both of them consenting
To marriage — and so forth.
To end the feud — and so forth.
They swear to tear the wall apart and live in
harmony!

The lovers
Are kissing.
The parents reminiscing.
The scene is one of utter bliss,
With not a cliché missing.
There's laughter—and so forth.
A happy dance—and so forth.
Then all at once a harpist and piano start to play!

BELL: I hear it!

HUCK: He hears it!

BELL: How beautifully they play!

FATHERS &
(EL GALLO): Drama!
(Just stick with me)

That's what he's offering; it's drama!
   (And you will see)
Into life's faded cyclorama,
   (How it could be)
He tries to shed a little light!
   (It's so exciting
    When you shed a little light.)

Thrilling!
   (It's ecstasy!)
We must admit that this is thrilling!
   (Such fantasy!)
And it can happen if we're willing
   (Don't you agree?)
To just make sure the price is right.
   (So why should you be pikers?
   Just make sure the price is right.)

FATHERS: Why should we be pikers?
Let's make sure the price is right.

(*MUSIC as the FATHERS dance.*)

BELL: It's so Spanish. That's why I like it!

HUCK: I like it, too! Ai yi yi!

EL GALLO: Who cares what you are spending
When you have a happy ending.

HUCK &
BELL: As the curtain is descending
It could really be heart-rending.

ALL
THREE: With a pretty rainbow blending
And with all our (your) friends attending —

Celebration!
Fireworks!
Fiesta!
Laughter!

Our (your) families are one!
There's joy ever-after!

And it all depends
On what we (you) —

HUCK: *(Speaks.)*
I say they're only young once. Let's order us a "First Class"!

EL GALLO
& FATHERS: *(Sings.)*
P-a-a-a-a-y!

Olé!

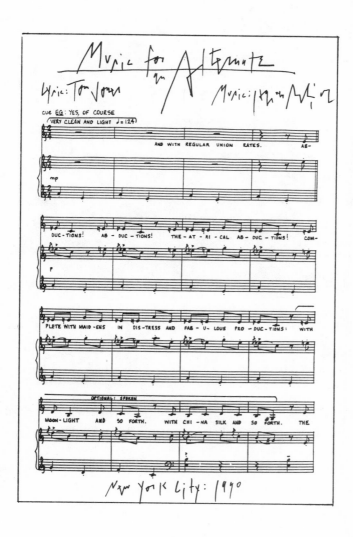

About The Producers

In 1970 Lore Noto took over the role of the Boy's Father, Hucklebee (opposite), a part which he played for sixteen years until illness forced his retirement in June of 1986. At first it was decided that the show would close, but after much protest from devoted fans, Lore's friend Don Thompson (pictured above in straw hat along with Noto in fedora) agreed to step in as acting producer, and the closing notice was withdrawn.

Long before winning an Oscar for Best Actor in "Amadeus," F. MURRAY ABRAHAM made his New York debut as Henry in *The Fantasticks*. He is pictured on the left with ROBERT GOSS as El Gallo, DON POMES as Mortimer and, in the background, FRANK GERACCI as the Mute, ERIK HOWELL as Matt and CAROLE DEMAS as Luisa, all three of whom are in the romantic pose above.

Memorabilia

R ITA GARDNER sings "Much More," at right.

Original cast photograph by Robert Benton (1960). Top: JERRY ORBACH (El Gallo). Standing, left to right: GEORGE CURLEY (Mortimer), KENNETH NELSON (Matt), RITA GARDNER (Luisa), THOMAS BRUCE (Author TOM JONES as Henry). Sitting, left to right: HUGH THOMAS (Bellomy), WILLIAM LARSEN (Hucklebee).

Pictured above are TOM JONES and JAMES COOK as the Old Actors in the 1990 Japan Tour. On their hands are puppets which Cook made especially for their Second Act scene as "Lodevigo and Socrates."

At left, GEORGE CURLEY as the original Indian and behind him, throwing the confetti, STANLEY JAY, who was the first replacement in the role of the Old Actor.

CARLA HUSTON, at right, who replaced RITA GARDNER as Luisa, tangled in during "Round and Round."

Pictured below is the abduction scene in a regional theatre production with SANDRA HOSSLEY, ED GELDART, AL TRAVIS and STEPHEN DALEY.

S ome of ED WITTSTEIN's earliest costume sketches for *The Fantasticks*. The ones above, for Bellomy and El Gallo, underwent substantial revisions before the opening, but the ones below, for Mortimer and Luisa, have remained the same, with only minor modifications (such as skirt lengths rising or falling), for over thirty years. The 1960 photograph on the left shows the costumes as they first appeared on GEORGE CURLEY as Mortimer, KENNETH NELSON as Matt, and RITA GARDNER as Luisa.

JERRY ORBACH and KENNETH NELSON cross swords as RITA GARDNER watches intensely. Shortly after this photo was taken, KENNETH NELSON broke his arm backstage during a performance. However, in true trouper fashion, he played the end of the show with the broken arm and showed up the next day to record the original cast album for MGM Records.

October 18 NBC-TV

At left, the great clowns BERT LAHR and STANLEY HOLLOWAY as the Fathers in the Hallmark Hall of Fame television production of *The Fantasticks* which was shown in October of 1964. Although shortened to less than an hour and presented minus Mute and Old Actors, the show was an enormous success and contributed greatly to the popularity of the Sullivan Street production in New York.

The complete cast is shown below, with RICARDO MONTALBAN as El Gallo, SUSAN WATSON as Luisa, and JOHN DAVIDSON making his television debut as Matt. The production was directed by GEORGE SCHAEFFER and choreographed by HERB ROSS.

Anniversaries

At left, after attending the Sixteenth Anniversary performance, Mayor ABE BEAM makes the first cut into the sixteen-tier cake. Pictured (left to right) are SEAMUS O'BRIAN, TOM JONES, MAYOR BEAM, JAMES COOK, SARAH RICE, HARVEY SCHMIDT, and LORE NOTO holding a special plaque from the City of New York just presented to him by the mayor.

In 1967, MARY MARTIN and ROBERT PRESTON, then appearing in the Jones/ Schmidt hit *I Do! I Do!* on Broadway, sent a special anniversary cake (below) down to their compatriots Off-Broadway.

In 1970, a company of *The Fantasticks* which was appearing at the newly-revamped Ford's Theatre in Washington, D.C., was invited to perform in the East Room of the White House (below). From left to right: GLEN CLUGSTON, KAREN GOLDBERG, GWYLLUM EVANS, PEGGY CLARK, LARRY SMALL, STEPHEN DOUGLASS, MRS. RICHARD NIXON, GUY GRASSO, and WILLIAM LARSEN.

The show's good fortune continued through the traditionally unlucky 13th year, and to help celebrate the event, producer LORE NOTO (left) is seen smashing a mirror under a stepladder.

t has played the White House!

Above: RICHARD CHAMBERLAIN as El Gallo and JOHN CARRADINE (in trap door) as the Old Actor in Chicago production.

Opposite page: Sullivan Street is renamed Fantasticks Lane. On the top of the ladder, SARAH RICE and, in descending order, JAMES COOK, SEAMUS O'BRIAN and CHAPMAN ROBERTS, with TOM JONES, LORE NOTO and HARVEY SCHMIDT on street level.

Drawing (above) by GROSS of CARLA ALBERGHETTI, JOHN GAVIN, TERENCE MONK, and EDWARD EVERETT HORTON, plus others in a Kenley Circuit tour.

Drawing (right) by DAVID GIBSON of GEORGE CHAKIRIS as El Gallo in a production for the Dallas Summer Musicals.

Drawing (left) by RONALD SEARLE for *Punch* magazine of STEPHANIE VOSS as Luisa and JOHN WOOD as Henry in the London production, 1961.

Caricatures

Drawing (below) by AL HIRSCHFELD for the *New York Times*. Clockwise, beginning at upper left: JAMES COOK and SEAMUS O'BRIAN as Old Actors, PHIL KILLIAN and SHARON WERNER as Young Lovers, ROBERT BRIGHAM as the Mute, HAL ROBINSON as the Narrator, and LORE NOTO and ROBERT TENNENHOUSE as the fathers.

Recordings of the Music

ED AMES
BURT BACHARACH
HARRY BELAFONTE
TONY BENNETT
THE BROTHERS FOUR
CAROL BURNETT
CHARLIE BYRD
PERRY COMO
RAY CONNIFF
BOBBY DARIN
JOHN DAVIDSON
BLOSSOM DEARIE
DUKE ELLINGTON AND HIS ORCHESTRA
ARTHUR FIEDLER AND THE BOSTON POPS
FOUR TOPS
ROBERT GOULET
MERV GRIFFIN
DON HO
KINGSTON TRIO
GLADYS KNIGHT AND THE PIPS
ANDRE KOSTELANETZ
PATTI LABELLE
THE LETTERMEN
LIBERACE
BARBARA MANDRELL
MANTOVANI
MABEL MERCER
LIZA MINNELLI
NANA MOUSKOURI
JIM NABORS
RICK NELSON
PETER NERO
ANITA O'DAY
ROY ORBISON
GEORGE SHEARING
BARBRA STREISAND
THE TEMPTATIONS
DIONNE WARWICK
ANDY WILLIAMS
ROGER WILLIAMS
and many others

Each spring, as *The Fantasticks'* anniversary approaches, composer HARVEY SCHMIDT has been asked to paint the show's logo on a new Chinasilk front drape as well as a new large sign out in front of the Sullivan Street Playhouse. 30 signs, 30 drapes.

He also designs the one small yearly ad which runs at anniversary time in the *New York Times*.

Director WORD BAKER, shown at left in front of the drape of the 1961 London production, directed a number of other early productions, including a touring company with LIZA MINELLI and ELLIOTT GOULD (above). Today he lives in retirement in his birthplace, Honey Grove, Texas.

Tom Jones' son Sam (age 3) understudying El Gallo, in Japan, 1988.

Early in the run of the show, when the houses were small but very often filled with celebrities, producer LORE NOTO contacted a lot of them about using their names in an endorsement ad (left). Twenty-five years later, he thought it would be fun to run that same ad again as part of that big anniversary ad campaign, but had to cancel those plans when he discovered that most of those same people were no longer living.

THE CITY OF NEW YORK
OFFICE OF THE MAYOR
NEW YORK, N.Y. 10007

February 1, 1990

To All In Attendance
1990 Japanese Tour
The Fantasticks
Tokyo, Japan

Greetings:

On behalf of the City of New York, which proudly shares a
Sister City affiliation with the great Metropolis of Tokyo, I
salute its citizens and His Excellency, Governor Shunicki Suzuki.

This is an occasion calling for a dual celebration. This is
the 30th anniversary of our Sister City relationship. We are
also marking the 30th anniversary of The Fantasticks, the
wonderful show that has attained historic status as the world's
longest running musical.

"Try to Remember" when it first opened...an entire
generation hadn't even been born! Accordingly, it is with the
hope of entertaining new audiences, as well as those who saw The
Fantasticks during its 1988 engagement, that these gifted
performers have returned to Tokyo.

May you enjoy their talents as much as they enjoy performing
for you.

Sincerely,

David N. Dinkins
M A Y O R

Members of the 1990 Japan Tour are shown below. From left to right: PAUL BLANKENSHIP, HARVEY SCHMIDT, RAY STEWART, MICHAEL PIONTEK, STEVE PUDENZ, RALSTON HILL (on floor), RICK RYDER, HILARY JAMES, DAN SHAHEEN, MARIE-LAURENCE DANVERS, HANK WHITMIRE (on floor), TOM JONES, JAMES COOK, NORMAN WEISS.

In 1988, after the Japanese production had been running for seventeen years, Jones and Schmidt were invited to take an English speaking company for a tour of Japan. This proved to be so successful that in 1990 they were invited to bring another company to Tokyo, Nagoya and Osaka. Since this marked not only the thirtieth year of the New York run, but also the thirtieth year that New York and Tokyo have been sister cities, MAYOR DINKINS was kind enough to write a special letter for the Japanese souvenir program. (Opposite page)

It has played al

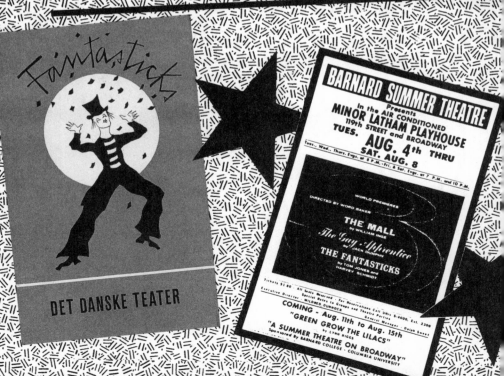

TEATRO DEL BOSQUE

RENE ANSELMO LUIS DE LLANO

presentan

"LOS FANTASTIKOS"

Una Nueva Comedia Musical

con

Armando Calvo   Ortiz de Pinedo
María Rivas
Guillermo Orea   Antonio Gama
J. Salinas   A. Pascual
y Alejandro Ciangherotti

Música de   Libro y Letra   Dirección:
HARVEY SCHMIDT   TOM JONES   LUIS DE LLANO

Dirección Musical   Escenografía
ENRICO CABIATI   DAVID ANTON

                VERSION ESPAÑOLA
Canciones: LUIS DE LLANO   Libreto: MARTHA FISCHER

HORARIOS: De Martes a Viernes una Función a las 8.30 p. m.
            Sábados dos Funciones 7.15 y 9.45 p. m.
            Domingos y dias festivos 5 y 8 p. m.
            Lunes No Hay Función

TODA LUNETA $12.00   NO HAY REVENTA

over the world!

Lilla TEATERN

presenterar

Fantasticks

genom *David Kushner*
En ny musical

TEXT   MUSIK
TOM JONES   HARVEY SCHMIDT

Översättning
GÖSTA RYBRANT

Musikalisk ledning   Dekor och kostymer
BO EKEMAR   GUNNAR LINDBLAD

Regi
JACKIE SÖDERMAN
TOM DAN-BERGMAN

Denna musical är inspirerad av en komedi av
Edmond Rostand

美国现代音乐剧

The Fantasticks

异想天开

・编剧 汤姆·琼斯
・作曲 哈威·史密特

中国戏剧家协会   美国尤金·奥尼尔戏剧中心
              联合主办
中央歌剧院 演出

-running musical,
...ticks,' ends June 8

...RA

...ne Fanta-
...tain. The
...usical will
...re than 26
...ormances at
...ullivan Street

...ano, I want to
...d producer Lore
...ow had to close
...re's no easy way
...re going out proud

...ormance will begin
...8, the producer said,
...rtly after midnight,
...thday.

...with this show since I
...re must be something
...lo," laughed Noto, who
...usical's financial condi-
...not as strong as in recent
...s not the major factor in
...end the run.

...n't come as a

surprise. We had discussed it with
Lore earlier this month. But it still
will be emotional." said Harvey
Schmidt, who along with Tom Jones,
wrote "The Fantasticks."

The musical is based on an obscure
Rostand play called "Les
Romanesques," a spoof of "Romeo
and Juliet." Two fathers invent a
feud to bring their children together.
The stars of the original production
were Jerry Orbach as the narrator,
Kenneth Nelson as the boy and Rita
Gardner as the girl.

The musical opened May 3, 1960
and cost $16,500 to produce at the
153-seat theater. The reviews were
mixed, but Noto, using part of his
own savings, had put by $3,000 to
keep the show running during that
first lean summer, and his persis-
tence paid off. Since its opening, the
show has paid its backers an 8,242
percent return on their investment.

Several factors prolonged "The
Fantasticks'" run. In its first struggling months, the show had dedicated

supporters including actress Anne
Bancroft and producer Cheryl Crawford, who called friends and urged
them to see the musical.

Singers like Ed Ames, Harry Belafonte and Barbra Streisand began
recording songs from the show, especially "Try to Remember" and "Soon
It's Gonna Rain," and the tunes
brought in new audiences.

In 1964, Noto allowed a television
version, which starred Ricardo Montalban, Bert Lahr, Stanley Holloway,
Susan Watson and John Davidson. Instead of hurting the show, the tele-
cast helped business, as did release
of production rights to stock and amateur groups.

The statistics are staggering: as
Jan. 1, 1986, 8,913 productions in
United States alone, including a
teur productions, and 472 pro-
tions in 67 foreign countries.

PLAYBILL

SULLIVAN STREET PLAYHOUSE

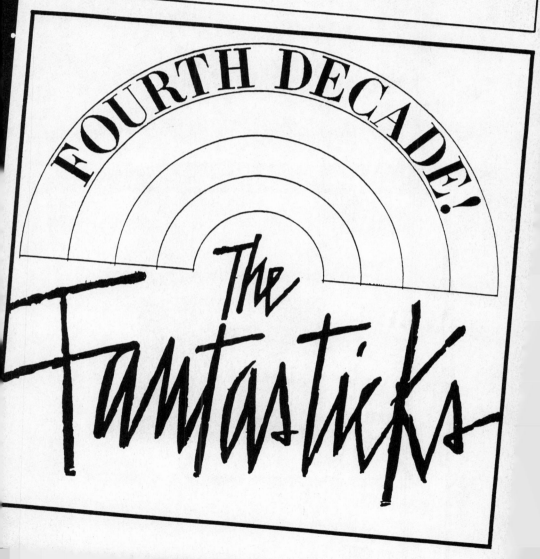

FOURTH DECADE!

The Fantasticks

STAGE DOOR

show
still
running?
LORE NOTO
presents
The Fantasticks
book and lyrics by
TOM JONES
music by
HARVEY SCHMIDT
directed by
WORD BAKER
settings and costumes
ED WITTSTEIN
musical direction
JULIAN STEIN

"A THEATRICAL WONDER"
Life Magazine

"DISTINGUISHED AND DELIGHTFUL"
Saturday Review

"IT IS STILL MAGICAL"
The Denver Post

"AS DELIGHTFUL AS EVER"
Variety

"FANTASTIC! INCREDIBLE! STAGGERING
Town and Country

"A MUSICAL PHENOMENON"
The Washington Post

*Tony Award & Drama Critics Circle
Award for Best Musical*

SWEENEY TODD: THE DEMON BARBER OF FLEET STREET

Music and Lyrics by Stephen Sondheim
Book by Hugh Wheeler

Based on a version of *Sweeney Todd* by Christopher Bond

Introduction by Beverly Sills

Here, with all its richness and power, is the monumental musical that revolves around the Fleet Street barber whose razor's swing takes many an unsuspecting victim and the woman who bakes them into pies. This thriller is as haunting to read as it is to watch on the stage.

"A work of such scope and vision and daring that it dwarfs every other Broadway musical that even attempts to invite comparison." — Rex Reed, NEW YORK DAILY NEWS

"*Sweeney Todd* is not just next month's cocktail party conversation — it will be talked about for years. This is sensationally entertaining theatre. Simply great." — Clive Barnes, NEW YORK POST

"*Sweeney Todd* stands head and shoulders above everything else in today's musical theatre." — Martin Gottfried, CUE

The Musical Library Edition of *Sweeney Todd* includes:

- Eugene Lee's set designs
- Franne Lee's costume designs
- Production photographs, cast lists and credits, and awards for all major productions, including the original Broadway production, the London production, the New York Opera production, and the current Broadway revival
- The complete discography

---

cloth • ISBN: 1-55783-065-7   paper • ISBN: 1-55783-066-5

Pulitzer Prize &
New York Drama Critics Circle Award

• APPLAUSE MUSICAL LIBRARY •

SUNDAY IN THE PARK
WITH GEORGE

Music and Lyrics by Stephen Sondheim
Book by James Lapine
Introduction by James Lapine

The young Georges Seurat was born in 1859 in Paris and died there in 1891. *"Dimanche, L'Après-Midi á l'Ile de la Grande Jatte"* ("A Sunday Afternoon on the Island of La Grande Jatte") was his second major work and *Sunday in the Park with George* is a work of fiction inspired by this masterpiece of Seurat and what little is known of his life.

Seurat, applying his grand artistic visions to canvas, neglects and abandons his mistress, Dot, who in turn runs off to America with a pastry chef. One hundred years later, Seurat's great-grandson, himself a struggling artist, returns to the island of La Grande Jatte, where Dot appears to him and helps him break through his creative block.

"Sunday is a watershed event that demands nothing less than a retrospective, even revisionist, look at the development of the serious Broadway musical!"
— Frank Rich, THE NEW YORK TIMES MAGAZINE

The Musical Library Edition of
Sunday in the Park with George includes:

- Tony Straige's set designs
- Patricia Zipprodt's and Ann Hould-Ward's costume designs
- Production photographs; cast lists and credits; and awards for all major productions, including the original Playwrights Horizons workshop production
- Lyrics deleted prior to the Broadway opening
- The complete discography

cloth • ISBN: 1-55783-067-3   paper • ISBN: 1-55783-068-1

Tony Award-Winning Musical
Based on the Plays of Plautus

• APPLAUSE MUSICAL LIBRARY •

A FUNNY THING HAPPENED ON THE WAY TO THE FORUM

**Music and Lyrics by Stephen Sondheim
Book by Burt Shevelove and Larry Gelbart
Introduction by Larry Gelbart**

Here in the fresh guise of an original story are the classics of slapstick; conniving slaves, overamorous young lovers, lecherous old men, domineering wives, seductive courtesans and bragging soldiers. What happens when a wily slave, Pseudolus, contrives to obtain a fair virgin, Philia, for his master, Hero, in the free-wheeling Rome of 200 B.C. is the basis of the antic humors concocted by Shevelove, Gelbart and Sondheim.

This classic musical script is surrounded by visual and literal arias of facts, photographs and illustrations to comprise the complete *Forum* experience destined for any musical lover's collection.

"A good clean, dirty show! Brings back belly laughs!"

— TIME

"It's funny, true nonsense! A merry good time!"

—Walter Kerr

The Musical Library Edition of *A Funny Thing* includes:

- Tony Walton's set and costume designs
- Production photographs; cast lists and credits; and awards for all major productions, including the original Broadway production, the London production, the 1966 United Artists Motion Picture, the 1972 Broadway Revival and other major revivals
- The complete discography

cloth • ISBN: 1-55783-063-0   paper • ISBN: 1-55783-064-9

Tony & New York Drama Critics Circle Awards for Best Musical!

A LITTLE NIGHT MUSIC

Music and Lyrics by Stephen Sondheim
Book by Hugh Wheeler
Introduction by Jonathan Tunick

A Little Night Music, suggested by Ingmar Bergman's film *Smiles of a Summer Night*, celebrates the ways of love on a turn-of-the-century Swedish estate and the Midsummer Eve follies of tangled liaisons and romantic intrigues.

"Heady, civilized, sophisticated and enchanting. Good God! An adult musical."

— Clive Barnes, THE NEW YORK TIMES

"Throwing caution to the winds, I assert that *A Little Night Music* comes as close as possible to being the perfect romantic musical comedy."

— Brendon Gill, THE NEW YORKER

"Like dry wine from a good year."

— Allan Wallach, NEWSDAY

"Here is real magic that bursts forth to engulf the audience."

— Rex Reed, NEW YORK DAILY NEWS

The Musical Library Edition of *A Little Night Music* **includes:**

- Boris Aronson's set designs
- Florence Klotz's costume designs
- Production photographs; cast lists and credits; and awards for all major productions, including the original Broadway production, the London production and the motion picture
- Lyrics deleted prior to the Broadway opening
- The complete discography

cloth • ISBN: 1-55783-069-X   paper • ISBN: 1-55783-070-3

the first time
in
American
Theatre
History

The
Fantasticks
tenth 10 year

sullivan street playhouse

The
Fantasticks
in its 19th Year!

181 Sullivan Street
OR 4-3838

The
Fantasticks

book and lyrics by
TOM JONES
music by
HARVEY SCHMIDT
directed by
WORD BAKER

sullivan street playhouse
181 sullivan

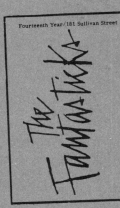

Fourteenth Year/181 Sullivan Street

The
Fantasticks

The Fantasticks

The
Fantasticks

FIFTEENTH YEAR
THE LONGEST-RUNNING MUSICAL IN THE WORLD
181 SULLIVAN STREET / OR 4-3838

The
Fantasticks

8

eighth year
at
181
Sullivan Street
OR 4-3838

The
Fantasticks

now in its sixteenth year
sullivan street playhouse
181 sullivan street

The Fantasticks

Celebration!
Fireworks!
Fiesta!
Laughter!

The
Fantasticks

Now celebrating its
30th Anniversary Year!
181 Sullivan Street/OR 4-3838

New York's
longest running hit
in
its
seventh
musical
year

The
Fantasticks

1 2
3 4

Fourth Year/181 Sullivan Street/OR 4-3838
The
Fantasticks

The Fantasticks

THE WORLD'S LONGEST-RUNNING MUSICAL
NOW IN ITS TWENTY-SECOND YEAR!

181 Sullivan Street

18

The
Fantasticks

now in its eighteenth year
sullivan street playhouse
181 sullivan street
OR 4-3838

now in its 13th
musical
year

181
Sullivan Street

The
Fantasticks

second year
at
181
Sullivan Street
OR 4-3838